Praise for *Eight Steps to Happiness*

'A beautifully written book. Inspirational, practical and built on a solid scientific foundation, it delivers what most self-help books only promise.

— Carol Kauffman, PhD, director, Institute of Coaching, Harvard Medical School

'This book is a gem. Drawing on the latest scientific findings *Eight Steps to Happiness* gives you the tools to make meaningful differences to your life. It offers that rare combination of being evidence-based, highly practical, and fun. Like the eight volunteers, you cannot help but emerge with more energy, focus, and happiness.'

— Dr Susan David, co-director, Institute of Coaching, Harvard Medical School and research affiliate, Yale University

'*Eight Steps to Happiness* is set to become *the* guidebook for increasing your happiness. Based throughout on what the latest scientific research is showing about how we can become happier, *Eight Steps* presents the simple practices we can use on a daily basis to increase our happiness. *Eight Steps to Happiness* will engage and inspire anyone who is looking for what it takes to build more happiness in their life.'

— Professor Alex Linley, author of *The Strengths Book* and founding director, Centre of Applied Positive Psychology

eight
steps to
happiness

the science of getting happy
and how it can work for you

Dr Anthony M. Grant & Alison Leigh

VICTORY
BOOKS

VICTORY BOOKS
An imprint of Melbourne University Publishing Limited
187 Grattan Street, Carlton, Victoria 3053, Australia
mup-info@unimelb.edu.au
www.mup.com.au

First published 2010
Text © Tattooed Media and Dr Anthony M. Grant, 2010
Photography by Dean Golja, © Heiress Films
Design and typography © Melbourne University Publishing Limited, 2010

Text design by Jenny Grigg
Cover design by Peter Long
Typeset by Megan Ellis
Printed by Griffin Press, South Australia

Page viii: 'Are you happy?' diagram © Dr Anthony M. Grant, 2010. Adapted with permission from the original by Alex Koplin and David Meiklejohn.

Page 42: 'Strategies to help you sleep' adapted with permission from Dr Craig Hassed's book, *The Essence of Health*. Dr Hassed acknowledges the prior work of Dr David Morawetz and his Sleep Better Without Drugs Program.

Page 110: 'Character strengths' from Peterson, C. & Seligman, M., *Character Strengths and Virtues: A Handbook and Classification*, Oxford University Press, Oxford, 2004. Used with permission of the VIA Institute on Character, Cincinnati, Ohio.

National Library of Australia Cataloguing-in-Publication entry

Grant, Anthony (Anthony M.)
Eight steps to happiness: the science of getting happy and how it can work for you /
Dr Anthony M. Grant and Alison Leigh

9780522858037 (pbk)

Includes bibliographical references and index

Happiness—Popular works
Self-actualization (Psychology)

Other Authors/Contributors:
Leigh, Alison.

158.1

Contents

Acknowledgements

We would like to thank all of the *Making Australia Happy* production team—especially Jennifer Cummins and Daryl Karp for their leadership, boundless enthusiasm and tenacity in creating *Making Australia Happy* and holding fast to a solid scientific foundation; Will Parry for his deft hand on the production tiller; Kalita Corrigan for her outstanding direction and dogged determination to tell the story; and Danielle Brigham for her ever-present collegiality and extraordinary research skills.

Thanks also for the knowledgeable and generous input of Anna-Louise Bouvier and Dr Russ Harris, whose professional expertise and commitment contributed so much to the series and the book. Many thanks to Daryl Karp and Foong Ling Kong from Melbourne University Press for their invaluable editing skills.

Most of all we would like to thank the Marrickville Eight for being so willing to put the science of positive psychology to the test in their own lives—and for having the courage to share their journey with us all with such openness, honesty and integrity.

For the Happy 100 Index, we are grateful to: Professor Lovibond for permission to reproduce the Depression, Anxiety and Stress Scales. Also to Dr Hendramoorthy Maheswaran, Professor Sarah Stewart-Brown and Dr Ruth Tennant for permission to use the Warwick–Edinburgh Mental Well-being Scale, which was funded by the Scottish Executive National Programme for improving mental health and well-being, commissioned by NHS Health Scotland, developed by the University of Warwick and the University of Edinburgh, and is jointly owned by NHS Health Scotland, the University of Warwick and the University of Edinburgh. We are also grateful to Professor Ed Diener for permission to use the Satisfaction with Life Scale. We also acknowledge the work of Dr N.M. Bradbum and the measurement of Affect Balance.

Dr Anthony M. Grant and Alison Leigh, October 2010

ARE YOU HAPPY?

NO

YES

DO SOMETHING DIFFERENT

DO YOU WANT TO BE HAPPY?

YES

NO

CARRY ON DOING WHATEVER YOU DO!

Introduction

This book, based on the ground-breaking ABC television documentary *Making Australia Happy*, is about happiness—the science of happiness.

We wanted to go beyond the rhetoric of motivational gurus and test the emerging science of Positive Psychology. Positive Psychology might look great in academic journals, it might sound good at conferences, but does it really work, and would it work on the streets of inner-city Sydney?

Our testing ground was the inner-west area of Marrickville. In a national survey of well-being the residents of inner-city Sydney turned out to have the lowest well-being in Australia.[1] At the epicentre of this inner-city area is the suburb of Marrickville. We figured that if our experiment can improve happiness here, it might just work for others.

We took eight volunteers from Marrickville, and with an expert coaching team we set out to see whether they could improve their happiness. We gave them brain scans, examined their minds, swabbed their saliva, reshaped their bodies and scrutinised their lives—all in the scientific pursuit of happiness.

The challenge was to improve their happiness and well-being radically over eight weeks. And to verify it scientifically. No nonsense. And it worked.

Now we have put all this experience into this book. In *Eight Steps to Happiness* we show how eight people from Marrickville went about improving their happiness over eight weeks using a simple eight-step program. And we show how this evidence-based program can work for you, too.

Eight weeks. Eight steps.

Part 1

Getting Started

Becoming happy

I t's hard to be happy. It's hard to be really happy. To stay happy. People let you down. The fates are unkind. Life conspires against you. The world grows cold and vicious. Life becomes bleak and grey.

Just when you think you've got it all worked out and it all seems in balance—just when you think, 'This is it! This is how I want to feel forever!'—the feeling slips away. Optimism and contentment dissipate. Anxiety returns. We get downhearted. We give up.

It's easier to go shopping. It's easier to find ways to make ourselves feel good by buying something new, going to the movies, eating nice food, drinking, getting on the internet, checking Facebook, other distractions. It feels good. But the hedonic treadmill—the vicious cycle of searching for material things to make us happy and ease our disquiet—is just that, a treadmill. We end up coming back time and again to the same place: discontent.

How can we break this cycle? How can we create sustainable positive change? Is real change even possible?

The habit of happiness

Positive change is possible. It is relatively easy to improve our levels of happiness on a daily basis. There is now a considerable body of scientifically validated techniques that improve well-being, that can bring increased happiness and meaning into our lives. People can change. You can change. You can do it.

But here's the rub. The inconvenient truth. You have to do it. And you have to do it yourself. And you have to get into the habit of doing it. Positive change works—but you have to work at it.

It would be nice if we could outsource our own personal development, to get someone else to do the work of change. Employ someone to put the effort in. And there is a veritable industry of motivational gurus, unqualified life coaches and alternative self-help specialists who offer instant personal change—'guaranteed'—as if by magic!

Unfortunately, there is no real short-cut. There is no magic bullet—but there is science. There are evidence-based approaches that work. What we have done in this book is to put together a simple, science-based eight-step program that has been shown to be truly effective at creating purposeful positive change. There is no bullshit. No sleight of hand. No magic tricks.

The key to creating purposeful positive change is to stick at it. It's easy to do something once. It's harder to do it twice, and even harder to stick at it over a period of time until it becomes a habit.

That's what is so useful about the Eight Steps to Happiness program. The eight steps in this book are all scientifically validated ways of improving happiness and well-being. They are designed to keep you engaged in the process over time. They offer new and varied experiences to help you move from insights to actions, from actions to habits. To help you develop the habit of happiness.

What is happiness?

Think of the word *happiness* and you might well visualise the ubiquitous yellow cartoon smiley face that has become synonymous with so-called positive thinking and the happiness industry.

But what does being happy really mean to you personally? Take a moment to think about a time when you were truly happy. Think about it. Chances are that you thought about times when you felt good—times when you experienced pleasure, you felt engaged—there was a sense of being connected, and you felt there was meaning to what you were doing. These three—pleasure, engagement and meaning—are the backbone of authentic happiness.[1] Happiness is a state of mind characterised by experiences of contentment, satisfaction, love or joy. Happiness feels good. It feels worthwhile. Happiness is pleasurable.

Is pleasure alone enough? Is pleasure happiness? There is considerable enjoyment to be had in activities like shopping, eating, drinking, self-gratification and the pursuit of pleasure of the senses. But unfortunately these are often followed by feelings of emptiness and meaninglessness. We all love hedonistic pursuits of this kind. And they can certainly boost our enjoyment levels and add variety to our lives. But on its own the pure pursuit of pleasure, the purely hedonistic life, is ultimately disappointing. There is a lack of richness and depth, the good feelings dissipate and we are left empty.

But the Pleasurable Life is only one part of happiness. The Engaged Life and the Meaningful Life are also important. These latter two are about eudemonism—an approach to happiness that emphasises doing the right thing, living in accord with your values, and experiencing fulfilment through the actualisation of one's potential. The Engaged Life is about owning your life—being able to make choices. It's about feeling that you are purposefully involved in life activities such as work, relationships and recreational activities. The Meaningful Life is about having a sense of purpose, living a life that is coherent and consistent with one's values, a life that is a source of satisfaction.

Happiness comes from having a balance between pleasure, engagement and meaning. It is not one or the other—you don't have to choose between being hedonistic or eudemonistic.[2] The lines between hedonistic pleasure and engagement in meaningful pursuits should not be drawn too tightly. In fact each influences and enhances the other. The research shows that feeling good, having positive feelings, tends to increase our sense of meaning, which in turns makes us feel good, and that this is further enhanced when we are engaged in the pursuit of meaningful goals in our lives.[3]

The happiness pie

What is more influential in determining happiness: the genetic influences of our parents, the amount of money we have and the life circumstances we find ourselves in, or choice—the intentional activities in which we engage? These three factors—genetics, life circumstances and choice—make up the 'happiness pie chart'.[4]

The research from large-scale, population-level studies show that genetics—heritable factors such as temperament—generally accounts for about 50 per cent of the difference between individuals. Life circumstances—how much money we have, where we went to school, where we live—generally accounts for about 10 per cent of the difference between individuals. Which leaves as much as 40 per cent of the difference in levels of happiness for intentional activities: the choices we make on a day-to-day basis about how we live our lives.

Each of these factors is important. And these percentages don't tell us about the absolute importance of each of these three sections of the pie for any single individual. This is because individuals vary. For one person, the genetic component might be highly influential, but their life circumstances might have less influence; the relative contribution of each section of the pie to one's happiness is going to be different for everyone. Nevertheless, the happiness pie chart provides a very useful reminder that our happiness is not pre-determined. Choice counts. We can choose to do things that will improve our happiness.

As we will see, there is a considerable amount of solid scientific evidence from philosophy, psychology, sociology, biology and recently from neuroscience to show that we can indeed improve our happiness. And there is good research to show that we can apply these techniques in our daily lives.[5]

The tyranny of the positive

Happiness is popular. Images of happiness are everywhere. Not long ago, the development of meaning in life and the pursuit of happiness was a private and, in many ways, a sober or profoundly personal quest.

Now you can go to happiness conferences. You can read more than 2000 academic articles on happiness each year,[6] buy hundreds of books on well-being, hire a happiness coach and even learn about happiness at university. Happiness has become truly mainstream— commercialised—and the proof is when Coca-Cola put the word 'Happiness' on its cans[7] and banks[8] use the 'Smiley' face in their ads and advertise 'happy banking'!

With the happiness surge in popular culture it might feel as if we are under pressure to be positive. We are exhorted to be happy, to be bright and bubbly—encouraged to be extroverted and confident. At work we are asked to demonstrate positive leadership, practise solution-focused thinking, maximise workplace well-being and create joyful, meaningful work. At home we read books on developing the happy family, and we watch TV programs about how to be happy. To some people it really seems as if we are bombarded by the relentless promotion of positive thinking—and some people end up feeling guilty about not being happy.[9] Understandably, some people are not very happy with happiness.

Is there no escape from the tyranny of the positive?[10] Do you have to be happy?

No—you do not have to be happy. And this book is not about forcing you to be happy. Happiness is not a panacea. In fact, so-called negative emotions such as discontent, uncertainty, disgust, anger and fear have a very important place in human experience. Tension, conflict and disagreement are vital parts of the creative process.[11] Pasting over the cracks of disagreement with the whitewash of so-called positive thinking or happiness compliance merely suppresses differences that are likely to surface in other, more virulent ways. We need to be wary of the happiness gurus who enforce black-and-white positive thinking.

Let's be clear. This is not what we are advocating. But if you do want to make positive changes, if you would like to enjoy life just that little bit more, then this book will help you. This book will help you make purposeful positive change and, just as importantly, help you recognise the times when it is best to practise acceptance, to be mindful.

Making the Eight Steps to Happiness program work

Change requires action. But our efforts at change are not always successful. All of us will have tried to make personal change in the past, only to find that the initial enthusiasm wears off as we slip back into our old familiar routines. Even though we are going to be doing things that will improve our happiness, we may find ourselves reluctant to do some of the exercises in this program. Having an understanding of the dynamics of change will help us stay on track.

The Transtheoretical Model of Change,[12] one of the most researched models of change, describes five stages of change. The first stage is precontemplation, where people are not thinking about change. The next stage is contemplation, where people become aware of the need to change, are thinking about making changes but have not actually done much about it yet. The following stage is preparation in which an individual's commitment to change increases. Individuals in this stage have had an insight about what they need to do. They intend to take action in the near future and may have started to make some small changes. For example, someone in preparation who wants to feel more energised and get fit might have checked out the local gym. Action is the stage where individuals make major changes—they are at the gym on a regular basis, eating healthy food daily, and enjoying the benefits of change. If these changes are maintained over a period of time, usually designated as six months, we can say that they are in the maintenance stage of change—the changes have become habits. Over time, people move from insight to action, from actions to habits. But, as we all know, relapse is very common. In fact most people will relapse—slip back to their old behaviour—several times before they consolidate change. And you can consolidate change.

Having a good overview of the change process, realising that change is not a linear process, and being clear that our motivation for change will fluctuate over time—and that is normal—these ideas help us to stick with the process. We don't have to get it perfectly right. If we feel ourselves slip away from the program, we just need to remind ourselves about the relapse stages and move back into action—review and renew.

Take a moment now. In terms of improving your enjoyment of life, which stage are you at? Where would you like to be?

Eight steps

The Eight Steps to Happiness program is designed to make change as easy as possible. You do not have to change your whole life to reap the very real benefits of this program. You only have to do a little bit at a time—one step a week is fine. And science is on your side.

The program starts with the end in mind. In step 1 you will write your own eulogy—a challenging but inspirational task. We then put the focus on other people in step 2 by looking at how acts of kindness can help other people and boost our own mental and physical well-being at the same time. Because we spend so much of our lives on autopilot, going mindlessly from task to task, in step 3 we explore the role of mindfulness in happiness.

Having developed our ability to be mindful, in step 4 we bring our attention to strengths and solutions—and the positive energy that they bring. Step 5 is about gratitude and appreciation, which are vital parts of the happiness equation: if we can't appreciate our lives and share that appreciation with others, then what have we gained? But we need to be open to other people if we are to make meaningful connections. Resentment and bitterness are toxic barriers to happiness. So in step 6 we learn about letting go of resentment and practising forgiveness. For some, this is a tough step. But we don't have to do it alone. Happiness is not a solitary pursuit. We are social animals—and happiness is contagious. So, in step 7, we look at the social determinates of happiness and develop social connections that will help us sustain our gains. Finally, in step 8 we take the time to reflect on what we have learnt, review our progress and renew ourselves in order to consolidate and truly develop.

Eight people

For the ground-breaking ABC television series *Making Australia Happy*, we found eight volunteers and, under the guidance of an elite happiness coaching team, we set out to transform them. Their brains were scanned, their saliva analysed, their bodies exercised and their lives examined in the scientific pursuit of happiness. Our challenge was to radically improve their happiness and well-being over eight weeks and to verify it scientifically.

Ben, 26, is the youngest of our volunteers. He loves music and his guitars. But Ben is stuck in a rut and he is desperate to get out of it—he just doesn't know how to start. When we met him he was struggling with the aftermath of breaking up with his girlfriend. He felt lonely, disconnected and unmotivated. He hated his job. Like many young Australians, he's massively in debt. Although part of

him knows that he has to come to grips with his life, he finds it much easier to go out and party—after all, there's always tomorrow—and Ben loves to party! Yet not facing up to his responsibilities is taking a toll on him. He feels isolated, lost and dissatisfied. As he sees it, 'I have never been very good at working out what I want to do next. I've never really had any, any goals or anything so ... so setting some goals is very important. I definitely need help in making some decisions, setting some goals, even little ones, and doing it. I want to be more assertive or more confident. I'd love to sculpt a life that I want to live instead of just going with the flow.'

Natalia is 34 years old. Single and looking for a partner, she really wants to fall in love, get married, have children, and give her life added meaning and direction. Her work as a social worker is stressful. She worries, and is a prisoner of a negative inner monologue that undermines her and colours her self-image and the way she presents herself to the world. 'I don't have a partner, and that makes me feel a bit like there's something wrong with

me. I would love to be able to let go of things from the past that are still haunting me, bad experiences that have definitely had an impact on my self-esteem and my ability to trust people. To be able to let that go would be fantastic because I know that harbouring that unhappiness is only doing me harm. I would also like to feel better about myself physically, and be kinder to myself, whether that's to do with adjusting my expectations on myself or having better coping strategies.'

Cade is 34 and lives with Matthew, his de facto partner of nearly eight years, in a small cottage with their beloved dog Callie. Cade is very shy. He becomes highly anxious in social situations, and describes himself as very moody, pessimistic and neurotic. Cade works as an on-air TV program scheduler, a role that—despite sounding artistic and trendy—is repetitive, boring and socially isolating. But there is another side to his life. Cade is extremely creative. Writing, photography, short films and music are his passions, and Cade spends long hours at night making short films and creating photographs. But the only place he feels comfortable displaying his creativity is online. His online creative work was good enough to be spotted and then exhibited by the Moscow Museum of Modern Art in Russia.

He'd like to make some changes—and he needs to. 'Being so afraid of social situations severely cripples my life. Life just constantly knocks me down and I get deflated so easily. I hold on to things and stress and worry about them. I would really like to learn how to manage my moods and adopt a happier outlook on life. I'd like to get into a more creative job. I've lost so much of my life being unhappy, it would be so wonderful if in the second half of my life I turned that around and really just experienced life and felt all the joy that there is to be felt in the world.'

Recently separated from her husband of twelve years, **Liz**, 35, is a mother trying to adjust to bringing up two young children on her own.

Although she loves her kids and loves to laugh, she feels unsatisfied and unfulfilled. She has a part-time job in sales, marketing and administration. Liz still deeply feels the pain of her mother's death nine years ago. A self-described gym junkie, Liz's extremely busy life involves perpetually juggling the competing demands of work, home, children and the gym while also trying to have a social life. She feels a real need to stay in control. 'I'm one of those people who thinks the glass is half empty rather than half full. I tend to look at what's not right as opposed to what's right. If I could change my way of thinking maybe I'd be able to open myself up a little bit more to accept that what I have is actually enough. Life can't go on in a mundane monotonous fashion. I really want to learn some strategies on how to deal with the situations that might normally really rattle me or make me feel sad. I need to know how to move on from the past mistakes and how to have a more positive outlook.'

Rebekah is on the eve of her fortieth birthday. As the mother of twin boys younger than three, her life is very busy. Married for twenty years, she is devoted to her husband and children. On the surface life is sweet, albeit hectic and exhausting. She finds escape and some time for herself through her running. Under the happy exterior there are painful issues she has never faced. She had a very unhappy childhood, and is angry

at her parents. She pours love and nourishment into her own family while at the same time pining for the nurturing that she had never received herself as a child. Like many people who had a painful childhood, she has pushed it to the back of her mind.

On one hand she is happy, full of the delights of life, energetic and passionate. But on the other hand she feels she has somehow lost her sense of resilience. Every day seems repetitive. She is ground down and exhausted. She wants to live a richer, more accepting, more meaningful life. 'I really want to be content, just being and enjoying, not self-examining or thinking about [the past] or catastrophising. I want to be present for my kids, and I want to find a balance so that it's not all just about them or about me. I want to find that reconnection with my life and myself.'

Tony, 42, is happily married with two children and owns a successful real estate agency. He has a keen sense of humour and is good at socialising, telling jokes, making you feel at ease—the life and soul of the party. He loves his family, his dog Dyson and hosting barbeques at home. He lives in a beautiful house with all the comforts of home. But he feels empty inside. The stress of running the business keeps him awake at night tossing and turning, and prompts bouts of dark moods and anger that lead to outbursts of rage—then the inevitable self-recrimination.

Tony would love things to change, to get rid of the dark empty feelings. He is fed up with his mood swings, his insomnia and his private worries. 'I get this pain in my chest, a feeling that I am worthless and that my life is meaningless. That's the scary part. I don't know what will happen if I don't do something about it. I would love to change for the sake of my kids and my wife. I hate upsetting my family and close friends. I'm still young and I know that I can do something to feel happy and good about myself again.'

Stephen is 51 years old. A former architect married with four children, he now works in sales and marketing for his wife's family business in architectural glass. He works long hours and puts in a lot of effort. He drives himself hard and is a perfectionist. Stephen struggles with work–life balance and finds it difficult to see how

he could reduce his working hours. He keeps himself buoyant, but there's always so much to do. He's unsure of his precise goals, but he knows that his life is way out of balance. He wants to be able to make better choices. 'I'd like to spend more time at home with the kids and be more available to the family, I guess, but I have a commitment at work and I get a lot of satisfaction from that. It's not more important than my family, but perhaps they perceive it that way. I'd like to be happier and to be happy more often so I can relate more positively to the people around me; I would like to have better understanding of my thought processes and how that affects my happiness, and I would like to learn to prioritise and find a better balance.'

Liz K is 63 years old and a retired scientist. She grew up in Scotland but has lived in Marrickville with her partner Nick for thirty-four years. They have two grown-up daughters. Having only recently given up work she is wondering what to do next. She loves her garden, doing Sudoku, reading and helping other people. Liz K is bubbly, talkative, vitally interested in life, politics and people and concerned that, as yet, she has not reached her

full potential. She feels that society does not value women of her age, and she is angry about that.

Liz K holds strong views. She cares about the world deeply. Her concerns keep her awake at night sometimes, worrying about issues like peace in the Middle East and Third World poverty. She wants to help make positive social change, but feels powerless in the face of global politics. 'I'd hate to think there was nothing ahead, [but] I'm not quite sure how to organise my energies. I think I give over a façade of being much more competent and cool than I feel on the inside. I lack confidence and self-esteem, though I am vastly improved on what I used to be. My head's a bit too busy, I'm [always] trying to sort out the world. I would love to feel a little bit more comfortable in myself, to get to a level of serenity. That would be a big plus.'

Our expert team were: coaching psychologist and team leader Dr Anthony (Tony) Grant, director of the Coaching Psychology Unit at Sydney University; Dr Russ Harris, GP, recognised expert in mindfulness and author of *The Happiness Trap*; and Anna-Louise Bouvier, expert physiotherapist, ABC radio presenter on fitness and Australian Fitness Presenter of the Year.

With the help of our team, the eight volunteers were ready to make changes, and throughout the book you will find out how they fared while on the program.

But reading about others is not enough. The Eight Steps to Happiness program is highly experiential and practical. It is designed to help you feel better, be happier and feel more like 'you'.

If you are ready to make changes, if you would like to have a bit more happiness in your life, or if you are simply curious about the science of happiness, turn the page and read on.

Challenging assumptions

'A science of happiness? You must be joking!' Fifteen years ago this would have been a common response. Today this is no joke. Hard-nosed and sceptical scientists around the world have been getting their teeth into one of the most subjective, contentious and deeply personal facets of human experience: happiness. Once the domain of philosophers or idealistic dreamers, happiness is now being studied by researchers in the areas of psychology, sociology, biology, and more recently neuroscience.

This new science, commonly called Positive Psychology, aims to discover and promote the factors that allow individuals and communities to thrive and flourish. It is the study of optimal human functioning, of what makes life most worth living—a science of happiness.[1] It forms the backbone of this eight-step program and the *Making Australia Happy* TV series.

Don't get us wrong. It's not that psychology was 'negative' before the emergence of Positive Psychology. Although scientists had been researching optimism, resilience, well-being, psychological health, goals and motivation for years, there was no specific discipline aimed at studying the positive aspects of human experience. Because of this, there was no simple way for the average person to come

Positive Psychology

In 1998 Martin Seligman, at the beginning of his term of presidency of the American Psychological Association, made the development of Positive Psychology his key initiative for his year in office. In January 2000 a special issue of the flagship journal *American Psychologist* published a special millennial edition introducing the notion of Positive Psychology. Edited by Professors Martin Seligman and Mihaly Csikszentmihalyi,* key figureheads in the Positive Psychology movement, the edition set out an initial agenda for this new field. Now the field has boomed. In the twelve years from 1998 to 2010 there were 4263 academic psychology articles on happiness cited in the database PsycINFO (the main psychology database) compared to only 2746 in the previous fifty years! The amount of research continues to increase each year.

* Seligman, M.E. & Csikszentmihalyi, M., 'Positive psychology: An introduction', *American Psychologist*, vol. 55, 2000, pp. 5–14.

by evidence-based information on happiness. That's what this book and the *Making Australia Happy* TV series is all about: taking science out of the lab and putting it into the main street. Making it accessible. For everyone.

Positive Psychology takes a broad perspective—a bigger picture. It looks at optimal functioning at many different levels, including the social, relational, institutional and cultural domains as well as at the personal and biological levels.

The field also challenges some common assumptions about happiness. For instance, does money really make you happy? Yes, and no![2] The rich are not happier. It turns out that once your fundamental needs are met and you can afford the basics— housing, good food, transport and the like—additional income does little to raise your levels of life satisfaction.[3] What about status? In fact well-paid professionals such as lawyers tend to have higher levels of depression, stress and anxiety than blue-collar workers.[4] How about work? Everyone complains about work—being at home must be better than working. Again—yes and no. It seems that people experience higher levels of 'flow'—a positive and very pleasant state of mind whereby people are totally absorbed in the present moment—at work than at home.[5] And work provides direction, meaning and purpose that gives many people a real sense of identity.[6] Surely sex makes us happy. Well, it's not quite the cure-all that we might think. One study found that having a bath or a shower was a more preferred way of boosting mood than having sex[7]—and for many people a bath might be far less complicated!

One clear finding from the sociological study of happiness is that the social context counts. It really counts. Our networks of family, friends and social connections have a major influence on our well-being.[8]

But how do individuals become happy? Can we just think ourselves happy? After all, we all have an incessant internal dialogue—a stream of self-talk—that creates meaning about our lives in the form of a narrative that comes complete with characters, storylines and subplot. Can't we just change the narrative and think ourselves happy?

Literally thousands of research papers indicate that we really can reduce depression and increase happiness by purposefully changing our thinking patterns.[9] And affirmative self-talk that helps us get into the right mindset to begin to work on our goals can improve performance on a wide range of tasks, including problem-solving.[10]

Much of the self-help literature would have you believe that just thinking about change will make change happen. Think positive thoughts, and positive things will happen. Think 'rich' and you will become rich. Just think happy thoughts and you will become happy. But this is not so. Unrealistic 'positive thinking' can do actually do some damage. One study that has major

Money and happiness

Although the rich might not be more happy, it turns out that how you spend your money is important. One four-year study found that spending money on purchases designed to create positive experience increased people's happiness.[*] The best way was to make a series of small purchases rather than one big one. Go to see a few local bands rather than splurge your money on one top-name music act. Spread these experiences over time. If you want to improve your satisfaction with your health, spend the money on experiences related to fitness, and do the same to other areas of your life. But stay within your budget. Overspending leads to stress and reduces happiness.

* Zhong, J.Y. & Mitchell, V.-W., 'A mechanism model of the effect of hedonic product consumption on well-being', *Journal of Consumer Psychology*, vol. 20, 2010, pp. 152–62.

Positive thinking

One study found that it was far more effective to use moderately positive statements involving specific personal attributes such as 'I love and care for those around me' rather than sweeping global statements such as 'I am a loving person and I warmly embrace the whole of humanity'.[*] Make it real! Remember, if it sounds too good to be true when you say it, then it probably is!

[*] Wood, J.V., Perunovic, W.Q.E. & Lee, J.W., 'Positive self-statements: Power for some, peril for others', *Psychological Science*, vol. 20, 2009, pp. 860–6.

implications for the scientific use of positive thinking found that people with low self-esteem—the very people most in need of a boost—actually felt worse about themselves after repeating so-called positive thinking statements such as 'I am powerful and strong and nothing in the world can stop me'.[11] By contrast, positive self-statements did provide a boost for people with high self-esteem—but the boost was quite small. The researchers suggested that if people with low self-esteem try to use so-called positive thinking to block out negative thoughts, they end up unintentionally reminding themselves that they don't actually meet the standards they have set themselves.

Our positive self-talk needs to be realistic. We can't fool ourselves.

But while we can't bludgeon ourselves into being always happy and positive, there is one thing that is just as important in making us happy as what we do, feel or think—and that is attention. Focus. It turns out that where and how we place our attention has a profound influence on our happiness.

Attention is the key

Attention is the process of focusing our mind on specific aspects of our experience while ignoring other things. Our attention is rather like a radar or spotlight. As we go through our day our attentional radar sweeps the environment picking up clues or signs that might be important to us, and our brains then are programmed to be drawn in to focus on specific factors. This happens automatically. Imagine if we had to stop to think all the time about where we should focus our attention. This automatic attentional mechanism is really useful as it minimises the amount of conscious effort we need to exert. It also has important implications for a science of happiness—and for unhappiness.

It has long been known that people with high levels of anxiety tend to have an attentional bias towards threat;[12] that is, anxious people automatically tend to focus on events that might be dangerous or threatening in some way, and they also interpret ambiguous information as being threatening.[13] For example, someone with a spider phobia is more likely to quickly spot the word *spider* among a long list of different words than someone without a spider phobia. And they are more likely to interpret a squiggly drawing as being a spider.

Our attentional bias can be so strong that, even when looking for a solution, we tend to lock on to the first solution we find, and our mind then directs our attention towards new information that supports our first decision and away from new or inconsistent information. This bias occurs even when we believe that we are looking for alternatives and new ideas.

Whatever grabs our attention can have an important influence on our well-being. This all happens unconsciously,[14] even before we have enough time to make a conscious evaluation or interpretation of the situation, and well before our self-talk begins.

However, we can make choices that change our attentional biases over time. We can purposefully refocus on things that are going to help us improve our happiness. We can focus our attention on the positive rather than being sucked into the negative. And the more we

Attentional bias

One study tracked the eye movements of chess players as they tried to solve a chess problem and found that, despite the players explicitly stating that they were looking for alternative solutions, their eyes tended to dwell automatically on the squares and chess pieces involved in the already familiar solution— even though they believed that they were actually looking for new alternatives!*

* Bilalic, M., McLeod, P. & Gobet, F., 'The mechanism of the *Einstellung* (set) effect', *Current Directions in Psychological Science*, vol. 19, 2010, pp. 111–15.

pay attention to the positive, the more we tend to notice. Attention changes our brains.

Happiness, mind and brain

Purposefully paying attention to the world around us by stopping to be aware of everyday experiences is one of the most powerful ways of cultivating a state of well-being. We don't have to be purely at the mercy of a restless and unruly mind. We can train our minds to focus on the positive by being mindful.

Mindfulness is a mental state of awareness that helps us live more consciously by opening the senses and focusing attention on the here and now.[15] It enables us to reduce the influence and effect of unhelpful thoughts and difficult feelings, and enables us to live with them while fully engaging in the present moment.

It has taken Western medicine a long time to acknowledge and accept what the Eastern mystics have known for thousands of years— that practising meditation and mindfulness can improve our well-being and even help to reduce physical pain. In scientific studies, mindfulness has been associated with lasting decreases in a variety of stress-related physical symptoms, including chronic pain; significant decreases in anxiety and depression; improved concentration and creativity; improved immune system functioning and decreased symptoms secondary to cancer.[16]

Even so, Western scientists were sceptical because they had no way of explaining what was going on in the reported behavioural and clinical effects of mindfulness practice. But in the last five years or so cutting-edge neuroimaging techniques have allowed scientists to look at computer-generated images of how our brains function in real time. Study after study is providing a growing body of objective neurological data that tracks the influence of state of mind on brain activity.[17]

Brain imaging is giving us a 'view from the inside' on how and why mindfulness and other aspects of positive psychology work.

We can now see which areas of the brain 'light up' when doing particular activities. For example, we now know that altruism triggers the same reward circuits in the brain as pleasurable activities like sweets or positive social contact.[18]

By scanning the brains of Buddhist monks who have individually clocked up tens of thousands of hours of meditation practice, scientists have shown that as a direct result of their meditation there is an altered pattern of brain activity in the part of the brain associated with regulating emotion.[19] Since those first experiments in 2004, there is now sufficient evidence to demonstrate that meditation is a unique state—distinct from resting states—and that it appears to promote long-term structural and functional changes in brain regions important for performing clinically relevant functions.[20]

Although tens of thousands of hours of meditation might be far more than most people can aspire to, recent research shows that we don't have to dedicate our lives to meditation in order to reap the benefits. Even as little as thirty minutes daily may improve attention and focus for those with heavy demands on their time and attention.[21] And it need not take long to learn these skills. Four days of training for only twenty minutes each day has been shown to significantly improve critical thinking skills and performance over a wide range of cognitive tests.[22]

Meditation

Research in this area is new. The first study to examine how brief periods of mindfulness meditation can improve specific subcomponents of attention, including the ability to prioritise and manage tasks and goals, the ability to voluntarily focus on specific information and the ability to stay alert to the environment, was published only in 2007. Simulating the workplace environment, volunteers who practised mindfulness meditation completed a range of different tasks at a computer that measured response speeds and accuracy. The results suggest that mindfulness meditation, even as little as thirty minutes daily, can improve attention and focus for those with heavy demands on their time and attention.*

* Amishi, P., Jha, J.K. & Baim, M., 'Mindfulness training modifies subsystems of attention', *Cognitive, Affective and Behavioral Neuroscience*, vol. 7, 2007, pp. 109–19.

So, if you want to make positive change, the research shows that it can be done. We have choice. We can change our thinking. We can train our brains. We can fine-tune our focus, and we can develop more positive and rewarding attentional habits.

Let's get started.

Making changes

I f we want to improve our well-being, be happy or create any positive change, there are five domains of human experience that we need to take into account in order to maximise our chances of success.

First, and most obviously, we need to know what to do—we need to make changes to our *behaviour*. Second, we need to have *thoughts* that support us in making change—constantly doubting our ability to make changes could stop us from even beginning to move towards our goals. Third, our *feelings or emotions* are powerful factors in motivating change—high levels of anxiety would not be helpful. Fourth, the *situation or the environment* that constitutes the social context we live in has a major influence on our ability to create purposeful change—trying to learn meditation in a very noisy or distracting place would not be a great idea for most of us. Fifth and finally, our *physical bodies*, or physical and biological states, have a major influence on our well-being and how we can use our attentional capacities. If we are not eating well, not getting enough sleep, have hormone imbalances or other chemical imbalances or even low blood sugar for example—these biological problems will place significant limitations on our ability to reach our happiness potential.

If your goal is to be happier ask yourself:

- How does your current environment (or situation) support you in reaching your goal?
- What are you doing to help you reach your goal? What could you do differently?
- What are you thinking, and how does that impact on your feelings and behaviour?
- Are you getting enough rest, nutrition, recuperation? What changes need to be made?

To benefit fully from the Eight Steps to Happiness program you need to be ready for action.

Motivation and goals

We need motivation if we are to create purposeful positive change. Some people think of change as a simple decision to do something different. In reality it is a far more complex process. Motivation is key. The word *motivation* comes from the Latin word *moveers*, which means to move, to be in motion. We can think of motivation as 'emotions in motion'.[1] Motivation, then, is movement. It is not sitting and thinking; it is about doing—action—as our volunteers discovered. But the reality is that the intensity of our motivation fluctuates considerably from one time to another. This is normal. Ambivalence is normal.[2] It is OK to have mixed feelings about change. You don't have to be 100 per cent committed—51 per cent is enough. What you do need to do is to get into action, and one way to get started along the path is to set a goal.[3]

All our volunteers started out by establishing values and setting goals. Setting goals gives us a direction to move in, a pathway to follow. It can be motivating to have a clear mental picture of what we want to achieve, as well as being clear about what we don't want. More than forty years of research shows clearly that, if we have a goal to aim for, we are far more likely to succeed.[4] There is more on goal-setting in Step 1: Goals and values.

Keep on track for change

To stay on track for change we need to keep track of our progress along the path. People who track their progress and keep a written record tend to be far more successful in creating lasting change.[5] This works for a wide range of goals, including health,[6] work[7] and happiness.[8] Write it down. Keep a journal. Keep a diary. Make some notes.

Some people feel reluctant to keep a written record. If you are hesitant about writing, some notes about your journey in a journal or notebook will suffice. Push yourself to find ways that will work for you. It does not have to be handwritten. Maybe you could keep typed comments in your electronic diary on your computer. Maybe you write simple notes on pieces of paper that you can keep in your wallet or handbag. Maybe you could write in a notebook that you keep in the car. Be creative. Writing it down really does help. Try it.

The body basics

Think of yourself as a Ferrari. You wouldn't run a sophisticated car like that on inferior octane. You wouldn't let the battery go flat. And you'd probably keep it polished and gleaming like new.

We need to give ourselves a head start by nurturing our body as well as our mind. You need to take an inventory of your diet, your sleeping habits and how much exercise you do to ensure that you are in top form and ready to take on the challenge of the eight-step program.

Exercise

Human beings are meant to move. We've been upright and walking for millions of years—at least three million—a long time.[9] Over all this time our bodies have evolved into sophisticated motion machines. Yet for the last hundred years or so we've been inventing

Exercise and happiness
How does exercise make us happier? Exercise increases serotonin, our main mood enhancing neurotransmitter. But there are many factors at play. When we exercise hard we stop ruminating on our worries and concerns, and we release pent up anger and frustration. Exercise helps us sleep better, and that also improves mood.[*] If you can, find somewhere green and pleasant to exercise. Studies show that we can further lift our mood by choosing to exercising in natural surroundings, whether urban parks or beaches or the countryside.[†]

[*] Hassed, C., *The Essence of Health*, Ebury Press, Sydney, 2008, p. 291.
[†] Pretty, J., Peacock, J., Sellens, M. et al., 'The mental and physical health outcomes of green exercise', *International Journal of Environmental Health Research*, vol. 15, no. 5, 2005, pp. 319–37.

ever more ingenious ways of avoiding the inconvenience of standing up and moving about. The motor car gets us to work, to school, to the shops—to pretty much anywhere—so there is no need to walk. With the internet came virtual shopping and chat rooms—no need to leave the house. With remote-control TV you don't even have to leave your chair!

All this was supposed to improve our quality of life. But far from making us happier and healthier, sitting on our backsides is actually killing us. A recent Australian study reveals that those of us who watch too much television have an increased risk of premature death and of dying from heart disease.[10] Sitting glued to the box for an average of more than four hours a day increases your risk of dying by a staggering 46 per cent compared to people who watch less than two hours.

But watching television is only part of the story. The modern workplace is a potential danger zone. It's not unusual for people to spend three-quarters of the working day sitting in front of a computer screen or on the phone at work. We drink coffee and eat lunch at our desks. We even send emails to the next-door office! All in all, depending on our job, and whether we get out and about after work or flop into a chair when we get home, we could easily spend almost three-quarters of our whole day (70 per cent) sitting.[11]

New evidence suggests that the risk remains even if one goes for a thirty-minute walk each day, as per the World Health Organisation guidelines—it is just not enough to offset the cumulative effect

Too much sitting is bad for you

How do we know that sitting down for prolonged periods of time is bad for our health? Researchers at the Baker IDI Heart and Diabetes Institute tracked the lifestyle habits of 8800 adults and found that each hour spent in front of the television daily was associated with:

- an 11 per cent increased risk of death from all causes
- a 9 per cent increased risk of cancer death, and
- an 18 per cent increased risk of death related to cardiovascular disease.

This held true regardless of other independent and common cardiovascular disease risk factors, including smoking, high blood pressure, high blood cholesterol, unhealthy diet, excessive waist circumference and leisure-time exercises.[*]

Why does sitting for prolonged periods have such a devastating effect on our health? 'The human body was designed to move, not sit for extended periods of time,' says Associate Professor David Dunstan, lead author of the study. 'Even if someone has a healthy body weight, sitting for long periods of time still has an unhealthy influence on their blood sugar and blood fats.' The muscle contractions that happen as we stand and move about are an important part of the metabolic process. Moderate exercise like walking helps us to metabolise fats and sugars, thus keeping the blood levels lower. It also increases blood flow and lowers blood pressure during and after exercise and stimulates immunity. All this adds up to a lower risk of many illnesses, including cardiovascular disease. When starting with an exercise program, it is important to start at a level you are comfortable with and gradually build up over time.

[*] Dunstan, D.W., 'Television viewing time and mortality: The Australian Diabetes, Obesity and Lifestyle Study (AusDiab)', *Journal of the American Heart Association*, 12 January 2010; Thorp, A. & Dunstan, D., *Stand Up Australia: Sedentary Behaviour in Workers: Baker IDI Heart and Diabetes Institute*, University of Queensland and Medibank Private, 2009.

of all that sitting. This might be surprising news for 'active couch potatoes'—those virtuous souls who think they can stay fit by following that golden thirty-minute rule and sitting for the rest of the day—but their health risks are as high as people who do nothing. You've got to keep moving!

Facing facts

We suspected that our volunteers were a sedentary bunch—which would go part of the way to explaining why they were not in good shape physically or mentally. To find out just how bad they were, we

Monitoring physical activity

In order to monitor our volunteers' levels of physical activity in minute detail we asked them to wear a SenseWear® armband around the clock. In addition to recording motion, SenseWear® measures surface skin temperature, sweat levels and body heat. This is considerably more sophisticated than a simple accelerometer that picks up movement but cannot distinguish between the intensity of the different activities. The armband recorded exactly how much or how little each of our volunteers moved, how much energy they burned, how long they slept and even the quality of their sleep. You will find more information in Part 3: Behind the Program.

asked them all to wear a sophisticated armband sensor that could tell us not only how much they moved but also how intense the movement was—even in their sleep.

The data revealed that most of the volunteers were 'active' couch potatoes, but two of them were straight-out couch potatoes who hardly moved at all.

Natalia was sedentary for an average of fifteen hours a day. Apart from the occasional game of tennis she was doing minimal exercise. To make matters worse, she was spending most evenings in front of her TV or laptop. Added up over the year she spent the equivalent of 229 full days sitting down—working, driving, watching TV or using the computer.

Cade was even worse. A self-confessed computer junkie, he was clocking up sixteen sedentary hours a day on average, mostly at his desk or computer. He admitted that he had never been one for exercise, and hated walking! When you added up all his hours, Cade was sedentary for the equivalent of an extraordinary 242 days a year.

'If you want to be happy you have got to get on your feet and challenge your body,' our program mind–body expert Anna-Louise Bouvier told them. 'Research is showing that a little bit of physical stress makes you more resilient to emotional stress.'

First and foremost most of us have to sit less and move more. Whether at work or relaxing at home, we need to find reasons to stand up and move about frequently. Standing up and bearing our body weight for just two minutes at a time at least once every hour is enough to trigger the physiological processes that keep our bodies in good working order.

Setting your exercise goal

We should all be aiming to walk 10 000 steps a day as an overall goal.[12] Ten thousand steps is roughly eight kilometres or 90 to 100 minutes of walking, but the idea is to accumulate those steps throughout the day rather than doing it in all one hit. Every little bit counts, even answering the door or checking the mailbox. A busy mother rushing to and from school and back and forwards to and from the shops might well accumulate 10 000 steps without even going for a formal walk.

Couch potatoes might be currently doing as few as 3000 to 4000 steps a day, so you need to create strategies to build up to the target as your energy and fitness levels increase. A combination of standing up and walking around plus a brisk thirty-minute walk five days a week is the most effective regime.

But walking ain't just walking! There's strolling, meandering, taking your time-to-get-there walking, and then there's the more energetic walking—the moderate to vigorous style of walking. It's the latter we're after. Moderate or vigorous walking is the key. Sauntering along isn't good enough. Put some effort into it!

The breath test

If you don't know what's moderate and what's vigorous exercise, take the breath test.

The breath test is this: if you can talk and sing while you are walking it's not energetic enough. You need to step up the pace. If you can talk but you are too puffed to sing, then your heart is pumping away at a moderate level. Once you become too puffed even to say a few words, you've reached the vigorous stage. Your lungs are busy supplying oxygen to your working muscles; there's nothing left over for talking.

Ideally, you need to be somewhere in the middle, between moderate and vigorous, to really benefit from the walk. Go for it!

Taking action

Natalia had a real wake-up call the day that she received the first results of her armband data. 'To hear that out of the course of a year I would be spending 242 days either sleeping or sitting was truly frightening and disgusting. It was very motivating and I came home that night like a wild thing and spent an hour and a half gardening and raking and anything I could think of to keep moving.' Anna-Louise set Natalia the challenge of increasing her moderate exercise during the week as well as at weekends.

Cade was instructed to build up his step count by walking to and from the railway station, and by resisting the easy option of taking the shuttle bus between the station and his office. He was also to take his dog for a walk every evening.

In addition to moving and walking, the rest of the volunteers were encouraged to take up an activity that would help to improve their mood as well as increase their step count. Tony needed an outlet to burn off his frustrations. In his youth he had been a gym junkie and a serious athlete. Anna-Louise suggested a weekly session of boxing—one of the most physically challenging activities you can do. Liz K, the oldest member of the group, was introduced to a series of exercises to build up her muscle strength, and also encouraged to take up ballroom dancing, something she and her partner had enjoyed years before.

Monitoring your progress

People frequently exaggerate the amount of exercise they think they have done. Our selective biases unconsciously focus our attention on what we have done—and magnify it!

Let's get real about this. To accurately monitor the number of steps you do each day, invest in a cheap pedometer. It works as an incentive as well as a task-master. People who wear a pedometer walk—on average—an extra 2.5 km a day.[13]

The pedometer is not able to accurately monitor your step count when you are engaged in a range of activities like cycling, swimming and weight training. For every ten minutes of these activities you can add 1000 steps to your pedometer count (100 steps per minute). For vigorous work-outs like running or squash you can double the step count: 2000 steps for 10 minutes (200 steps per minute).

Ideas to get you moving

Here are ten great ideas from Anna-Louise to get you moving. Try to come up with ten more of your own.

- Get off the bus one stop before home, then two stops, then three and so on.
- Walk the dog once more round the block.
- Buy a newspaper from the corner store instead of having it delivered.
- Park the car in the corner of the car park furthest from the shopping centre.
- Walk up stairs instead of using the lift.
- Ban emails between colleagues in the same office between 10am and 3pm. Go and talk to each other instead. Fine those who break the ban and give the money to a charity.
- Take phone calls standing up.
- Move your printer away from your desk.
- Hold walking meetings. Why sit round a table when you can go for a walk?
- Take up an activity that you already love or you think you would like.
- Get into a routine and record your progress in your happiness journals.

Lack of time isn't an excuse not to exercise. If you want to live longer, sleep better and feel better, you must make exercise a priority. It's a small investment in the rest of your life—and for your happiness today.[14]

Diet and nutrition

Happy food?

Many of us turn to food to make us happy, but ironically the very foods we turn to are the ones more likely to make us feel worse. When was the last time you reached for a piece of salmon when you were feeling down? Comfort foods have their place but the comfort they offer is short-lived. In the long term they might even make us unhappy.

Diet and depression

The number of depressed people in the Western world is skyrocketing. By 2020 depression will be the second most common cause of disability in the world, second only to heart disease,[15] and our modern diet of processed foods could be partly to blame.

Researchers at Melbourne University have discovered a direct link between diet and depression. For ten years they monitored the diets of more than a thousand women and then measured their moods. Women on an unhealthy Western-style diet of processed or fried foods, refined grains, sugary products and beer were 50 per cent more likely to develop depressive symptoms. Women eating a balanced diet of vegetables, fruit, beef, lamb, fish and wholegrain foods were about 30 per cent less likely to develop depression and anxiety disorders.[16]

Another study in Spain of 11 000 men and women came up with similar results: people on what they called a Mediterranean-style diet rich in vegetables, fruits, nuts, whole grains and fish had a more than 30 per cent reduction in the risk of depression than those whose diet had lacked those crucial elements.[17]

Yet another study in the UK monitored the diets of 3500 people for one year. Five years later they found that—you guessed it—those in the group eating processed foods were more likely to show symptoms of depression than the ones eating wholefoods.[18]

So, is the food making them depressed or is depression driving them to that food? It is probably a vicious circle.

Chocolate, ice cream, cakes, biscuits, chips, hamburgers, sausage rolls, pizza, soft drinks: foods that were rare indulgences a little more than a generation ago have become the staple diet of millions of households. They are called 'junk foods', and for good reason. These foods lift the spirits temporarily. They give us instant bursts of energy. But the 'hit' doesn't last long. We end up dissatisfied and wanting more. More worrying is that a staple diet of junk food deprives the brain of essential nutrients,[19] which we require for physical and mental well-being. This could even be turning some of us into junk food addicts complete with the mood swings that addiction entails.[20]

It is clear that we can actually protect ourselves against depression by eating better foods. So, just like all the volunteers in the program, before you embark on the happiness program you really should take a long hard look at what you eat and be prepared to make changes.

Junk food can be addictive

Scientists at Princeton University and at Scripps Research Institute in Florida have separately shown that rats fed on junk food undergo neurochemical changes in their brains that mimic those produced by heroin, nicotine and other addictive drugs. Like drugs, the foods stimulate the cells that trigger the release of dopamine, followed by a pleasure hit. However, the hit is short-lived, and leaves the rats—and, by implication, us—craving more. The rats quickly develop binge tendencies, and if the food stops coming they get the shakes, just like drug addicts.[*]

[*] Johnson, P.M. & Kenny, P.J., 'Dopamine D2 receptors in addiction-like reward dysfunction and compulsive eating in obese rats', *Nature Neuroscience*, vol. 13, 2010, pp. 635–41. Avena, N.M., Rada, P. & Hoebel, B.G., 'Evidence for sugar addiction: behavioral and neurochemical effects of intermittent, excessive sugar intake', *Neuroscience and Biobehavioral Reviews*, vol. 32, 2008, pp. 20–39.

Cade's diet

When we first met Cade he lived exclusively on junk food. He did not eat a single fresh vegetable or piece of fruit from one week to the next. His breakfast consisted of a Kit-Kat and a can of Red Bull. For lunch he would have a bowl of pasta and another can of Red Bull. Another chocolate bar and a Red Bull for tea. A pizza for dinner ended his day. On Saturdays and Sundays he didn't have set meal times, but when he did eat to satisfy his hunger, depending on the time of day, it would be Fruitloops, sliced cheese on toast or pizza, washed down with 'lite' milk or chocolate milk, and an incessant supply of Red Bull. He supplemented his diet with over-the-counter painkillers to relieve headaches, which regularly started about half an hour after he got up.

Cade was an extreme case. That he was still walking and talking is little short of a miracle. He was physically inactive, had minimal contact with other people, and was constantly lacking in energy. No wonder he was unhappy!

Cade's body was like a car that was running on empty. Just as cars need petrol, the body needs glucose, a form of sugar, which it converts into energy. A car needs a constant supply of petrol to keep running; the body and the brain need a nice steady release of glucose to keep powering on.

The body gets its glucose from carbohydrates. The trouble with junk foods is that they contain so-called simple carbohydrates: sugars that break down into glucose so quickly that the energy boost is sweet but short-lived. Anna-Louise Bouvier calls it 'short energy fuel'.

Cade needed 'long energy fuel' to keep the motor running over long distances. This comes from 'complex' carbohydrates, which stay in the system longer because they convert more slowly into glucose. These are the components of the Mediterranean diet: vegetables, fruits, nuts, rice, wholegrains and fish. They are often referred to as low GI (low glycaemic index) foods, referring to the rate at which food breaks down into glucose. They don't supply that wonderful sugar hit, but equally you won't get that low feeling when that beautiful hit has done its dash.

Cade's diet was also devoid of omega 3, another essential ingredient of a healthy diet. We need lots of omega 3 polyunsaturated fatty acids to service the cogs and wheels of the human engine. Without it the parts start to fail. The trouble is that omega 3 is found in oily fish and wild game—and these have all but disappeared from the mass-produced Western diet. Instead we consume large quantities of unsaturated fats in farm-produced meat products. And we also eat high quantities of polyunsaturated omega 6 fatty acids. These are found in the vegetable oils that are used in fast food and snack food. We are flooding our human engines with omega 6, and that seems to be putting a serious spanner in the works.

Omega 3 plays a vital role in the processes that keep our bodies functioning, such as the growth of new brain cells and acting as an anti-inflammatory agent. Too much omega 6 can inhibit these functions and affect the ability of the brain cells to communicate with each other.

It seems increasingly likely that this imbalance of omega 3 and omega 6 is contributing to the meteoric rise in people suffering from mood disorders and depression. Evidence is growing that people who eat lots of fish are less likely to be unhappy or depressed than people who do not.[21]

Cade's appalling diet was clearly contributing to his lack of energy and constant headaches. Weaning him off his bad habits was never going to be easy. But instead of taking it slowly Cade decided to go cold turkey. He cut out all sugar, high-fat and high-energy food and drink, sending his body into revolt. 'I am ridiculously tired and lethargic,' he wrote in his journal, 'and headachy with nausea on and off. My body is screaming out for sugar and grease.' Cade was showing classic signs of withdrawal symptoms.

Whether there is such a thing as sugar addiction is contentious in scientific circles.[22] But call it what you will—addiction or dependence—many of us, like Cade, find it difficult to control our intake of sugary and fatty food. But now is the time to start. You don't need to go cold turkey like Cade. You don't need to follow a special diet. All you have to do is familiarise yourself with the Australian Dietary Guidelines,[23] and start to plan your menus around them.

Sleep

One of the casualties of living in a 24-hour, seven-days-a-week society, as well as having low exercise levels and a poor diet, is that it becomes harder and harder to get a good night's sleep.

Sleep matters

There is plenty of evidence that a poor night's sleep is a key driver of moodiness, and when sleep improves, mood improves. Before electricity, people generally slept on average about ten hours a night, from sunset to sunrise.[24] In the developed world the average is now about seven. You might think that you can get by on five hours sleep or less, but science tells us you need more. Good-quality sleep and plenty of it is a biological necessity. It is fundamental to our mental and physical health and well-being, as important as food and water.[25] Poor sleep or too little sleep lowers our quality of life and can even be a health hazard.[26]

Without sleep the parts of the brain that govern our emotions are disrupted, leaving us poorly prepared to deal with the next day's challenges and social interactions.[27] Chronic sleeplessness has been recognised as a symptom of depression for years, but now we know that it also works the other way round: it can also cause depression.[28] At the very least it will make us tired and emotional.

As well as playing havoc with our moods and our emotions, too little sleep reduces our ability to concentrate, impairs our memory and judgement and makes us more prone to accidents. Shift workers

Sleep affects your mood

A good night's rest can regulate your mood and help you cope with the emotional challenges of the day, according to a 2007 brain imaging study from Harvard Medical School and the University of California.[*] Losing a night's sleep has the opposite effect, boosting the areas of the brain associated with depression, anxiety and other psychiatric disorders.

People who had not slept for thirty-five hours were shown a series of images, some of which were highly emotionally charged. Using functional Magnetic Resonance Imaging (fMRI), the researchers were able to monitor how their brains responded compared to a second group who had enjoyed a good night's sleep.

In the sleep-deprived group, the brain mechanisms that regulate our emotions dramatically overreacted and lost the ability to rationalise and mitigate responses to the pictures, unlike the brains of a second group, who had had a good night's sleep.

The amygdala is the region of the brain that alerts the body to protect itself in times of danger. In the normal course of events, the prefrontal cortex, which commands logical reasoning, would recognise the images to be make-believe and would send out 'settle down' signals. Instead the sleep-deprived brain shut down the prefrontal cortex and thus prevented the release of chemicals needed to calm the fight-or-flight reflex.

[*] Walker, M.P., 'The role of sleep in cognition and emotion', *Annals of the New York Academy of Science*, vol. 1156, Issue: The Year in Cognitive Neuroscience 2009, pp. 168–97.

especially are at risk in the workplace and on the road. After twenty-four hours without sleep, their hand-to-eye coordination is affected to the same extent as having a blood alcohol count of 0.1. One in six road accidents is probably caused by lack of sleep. On country roads in Australia, it's as many as one in four.[29]

Our bodies are programmed to work on an alternating cycle of rest and activity. Sleep allows time for repair and growth. If the cycle is disrupted our health suffers. It's not so much how many hours we sleep that matters, it's the quality of the sleep. That's why some people can get by with five or six hours while others need seven or eight.

What causes poor sleep

There are all sorts of reasons why we can't sleep. Stress is a big one—worrying about work, worrying about money, worrying about the kids. Noise is another—a crying baby, the neighbour's TV, a snoring partner. The room may be too cold or too hot. The bed may be too soft or too hard. It may even just be staying up too late and drinking and smoking, which overstimulates the nervous system, making sleep more difficult. It could be that our internal body clock is out of phase.

Circadian rhythms

Sleep is regulated by circadian rhythms, the 24-hour cycles that regulate the biological and physiological processes of all living things. Our circadian rhythms are in-built biological programs that trigger the hormonal secretions and body temperature fluctuations that determine when we feel sleepy and when we feel alert.

Most people feel more alert in the morning and tend to become drowsy in the afternoon. We're alert again in the early evening, when our temperature is generally at its highest. When darkness falls, in the normal course of events, the hormone melatonin kicks in. Melatonin builds up to peak levels from 8pm to 10pm or 11pm, and as it does so our temperature drops and our bodies drift towards sleep. When daylight arrives in the morning our melatonin levels drop, our body temperatures rises and, if all is working to plan, we'll wake up feeling rested and alert.[30]

Going to bed at strange hours disrupts our biological clock. This forces us to push through the fatigue barrier at the same time as our bodies are telling us that it's time to sleep.

But whether the cause is jetlag, shift work or our own bad sleeping habits, if the body clock has become wrongly adjusted, we may be in the habit of not falling asleep until the early hours of the morning or waking up frequently through the night. This is a pattern that deprives us of deep sleep, and deep sleep is what sustains us.

Some sleep disorders are physical. Periodic limb movement, as its name implies, involves frequent involuntary movements that go on all night. Sleep apnoea is the result of a blockage in the throat that restricts breathing. People who suffer from it usually snore and snort like trains, but they often don't notice that they are being roused from sleep hundreds of times a night as they struggle for air. In both cases the constant arousal prevents the sleeper from sinking into deep sleep.

Poor sleep revealed

The armband data that we collected from the volunteers revealed that most of them were missing out on restorative sleep. More than half of them were regularly getting less than five hours quality sleep a night, often because they had spent too long in front of a light screen surfing the net until just before going to bed, in effect fighting their natural circadian rhythms.

Liz K was going to bed after 1am and waking at six after a night of broken sleep. Her problem was an overactive mind.

Ben's armband data revealed extremely erratic sleeping patterns. Some nights he was sleeping less than three hours a night. Even if he was in bed for six hours he was lucky to get five hours of sleep with all his tossing and turning. He was staying up late playing his guitar or calling up friends and going out because he was feeling lonely and isolated.

Tony was the worst sleeper in the group, averaging around four and half hours of sleep a night. He snored a lot and was waking up every twenty minutes or so. Consequently in the morning he was exhausted and grumpy. He could not remember when he had last had a decent night's sleep.

Tony's disrupted sleep looked suspiciously like sleep apnoea, a condition in which people repeatedly stop breathing during their sleep, sometimes for up to a minute at a time. Apart from leaving one tired and unrefreshed, sleep apnoea can be dangerous if left untreated. It's been linked to hypertension, which can lead to heart failure, stroke and other life-threatening conditions.

Strategies to help you sleep

- Exercise vigorously in late afternoon/early evening. Don't exercise strenuously immediately before bedtime.
- Don't nap too long and too late in the day. A short nap (less than 20 minutes) directly after lunch can be restorative. Longer or later than that and you reduce your chances of deep sleep at night.
- Cut down on alcohol. It helps you sleep initially but wakes you in the second half of the night and over time can chronically fragment your sleep.
- Avoid stimulants like tea, coffee and other caffeinated drinks before bed.
- Do something to relax, such as meditate or have a warm bath.
- Only go to bed if you feel sleepy.
- Stop reading, worrying or watching television in bed. Stop using the computer half an hour before going to bed. Limit your activities in the bedroom to sleeping and sex.
- If you can't sleep, get up, go to another room and do something else until you feel sleepy again.
- Get up at the same time every morning regardless of how much sleep you have had.
- If your brain is churning with worrying thoughts, write them into a notebook by the bed, and resolve to deal with them the next day.

After a visit to a sleep clinic, he was diagnosed with a mild apnoea. The specialist said it was not serious enough to need treatment, but advised Tony that he would probably sleep better if he did more exercise and lost some weight. He also recommended that he try some of the strategies listed (see box) to change his sleep patterns.

Get moving

Exercise is one of the best ways of helping us get to sleep, sleep longer and sleep more deeply. What we need is a vigorous workout, one that will keep the heart rate up and the muscles pumping continuously for at least twenty minutes. The ideal time to do this is late afternoon or early evening. If we leave it too close to bedtime we will be overstimulated just when we want to calm down. Our body temperature will be high just when it should be falling in order to trigger the onset of sleep.[31]

A good night's sleep in itself won't make us happy. The anxieties of daily life are still out there. But it does make it easier to manage the daily grind.

Be kind to yourself. Move more, sleep more and eat well. In so doing you will be oiling the wheels for your eight-step path to happiness, and you can expect a smoother, more comfortable ride.

Keep on track

It is really important to keep on track. Keep a record of your changes. Note your sleep patterns. Chart your daily steps. Write down your daily food intake. Get started. Set your goals, measure your change and you will improve—you will become happier.

Part 2

Eight Steps to Happiness

The Happy 100 Index

W hen making any type of purposeful positive change we need to be able to keep track of how we are going. We need to be able to monitor our progress. This section provides some tools to help you do just that.

We wanted to give our volunteers and our readers a simple but comprehensive way of measuring their happiness journey. We wanted the measure to be easy to understand, easy to complete and meaningful. Ideally, and in order to make it really easy to understand, we would have just a single number that would represent progress. But doing this had a number of challenges.

First, whether we can boil happiness down to a single number is controversial. On one hand psychologists tend not to want to do this because such reductions can oversimplify complex psychological concepts. On the other hand, measures such as IQ—which does use a single number, and does reduce the highly complex concept of intelligence to one number—is widely used by psychologists and the general public, and it is very useful and well accepted. Maybe we could do the same for the measurement of happiness.

Second, this program works by reducing stress, anxiety and depression as well as boosting happiness. So we would need to measure the presence (or absence) of stress, anxiety and depression as well as the presence (or absence) of happiness.

Third, there are many different questionnaires that measure happiness and well-being, as well as questionnaires that measure anxiety, stress or depression. Some are very complex. Some require a psychology or medical degree to use. Not all of these questionnaires are suitable for use with the general public—many are designed for use with severely depressed or psychiatric patients, and this program is designed for the average person—not people with major mental health problems. Which questionnaires would be the best for us to use?

Fourth, the questionnaires had to be scientifically validated. This program is science-based. There's no nonsense. No wishful thinking. It is grounded in evidence-based Positive Psychology. The questionnaires had to be good. They need to work, and work well.

How best to deal with these concerns? We went back to the drawing board, back to basic theories of happiness, to see what the research literature said about happiness.

If we could divide happiness into its different component parts and identify the different mental health issues related to happiness, we might be able to bring together a number of good, previously validated questionnaires. Ideally we would end up with a short composite measure—a measure that combined a number of related aspects of mental health in a way that could give us a single meaningful happiness score.

The structure of happiness

The nature and structure of happiness has long been debated. In the past philosophers have tended to separate happiness into two key concepts: hedonic well-being—the pleasurable life—and eudemonic well-being—the meaningful life. But recent work by Positive Psychologists has moved beyond this somewhat simplistic division to include the notions of *subjective well-being* and *psychological well-being*.

Subjective well-being has two components: an emotional component, which includes both positive and negative feelings, and a cognitive component: rational judgements or evaluations about the quality of our lives, that is, how satisfied we are with our lives. Happiness from this perspective results from a balance between positive and negative emotions and takes into account how satisfied we are. Positive emotions include joy and contentment, and negative emotions include feeling depressed or anxious. If we have more positive than negative emotions then we are more happy than not.[1] And greater satisfaction leads to greater happiness.

Psychological well-being, on the other hand, focuses more on concepts such as personal growth, acceptance, being able to make meaningful choices and having a purpose in life. It focuses more on one's mental well-being than one's feelings or emotions. Both subjective and psychological well-being are vital parts of happiness.

With permission from the original authors we used previously well-established and scientifically validated questionnaires that measured all these aspects of happiness. We then followed the ideas for measuring happiness proposed by some of the leading researchers in Positive Psychology.[2] Because subjective well-being and psychological (or mental) well-being are very closely related,[3] we used them both. We also included questionnaires that assessed anxiety stress and depression. The result is a short comprehensive questionnaire that incorporates all the main aspects of happiness. It is not the definitive assessment of happiness, but is it very useful. And it works.

Measurement?

But can happiness really be measured? If we mean can we achieve a truly objective assessment of happiness, in the same way that you can objectively measure your height or weight, then the answer must be 'no'. But happiness is not weight or height. It is a subjective experience. And we can reliably measure what people *think* about how happy they are. We can reliably measure their subjective evaluations. There are literally thousands of research studies, from individual to whole country populations, that have measured happiness this way. However, to get the most out of this it is important that you complete these questionnaires frankly and honestly. Don't try to fake it. You'll only be fooling yourself.

We have designed the Happy 100 Index so that if you score 50 you are neither happy nor sad overall. You are neutral. With a score of 50 you could have a high level of positive feelings and at the same time have a high level of negative feelings. This is possible and relatively common. A score of 50 means that your happy and sad scores balance each other. If you have a score greater than 50 then overall you are more happy than sad. A score of less than 50 means you are more sad than happy. Drawing on much previous research into well-being and happiness,[4] we would expect the average Australian to score about 70 to 75 on the Happy 100 Index—that was our benchmark on the series.

The Happy 100 Index is meant to be used to help you gauge your progress. You can take it once a week or even every couple of days. Keep a note of your score. This is not a competition. Don't try to compare yourself to other people. Use this to better understand yourself and to keep on track. This is to help you reach your personal happiness goals, not to be better than other people.

Note that the Happy 100 Index data is for general information only and should not be used for self-diagnosis. It is not possible to determine whether someone suffers from depression, anxiety or excessive stress on the basis of a score from the Happy 100 Index. You should see your GP or a qualified mental health professional if you have any concerns about your Happy 100 Index score or are worried about your mental health.

Happy 100 Index

Section A

Please read each statement and circle a number 0, 1, 2, 3, 4, 5 which indicates how much the statement applied to you *over the past week including today*. There are no right or wrong answers. Do not spend too much time on any statement. To get an accurate result you must answer each question honestly. Read each question carefully.

The rating scale is as follows:
0 Strongly Disagree: This did not apply to me at all (Not at all)
1 Disagree
2 Slightly Disagree
3 Slightly Agree
4 Agree
5 Strongly Agree: This applied to me very much (nearly all the time)

		Not at all					Nearly all the time
1	I've been feeling optimistic about the future	0	1	2	3	4	5
2	I've been feeling useful	0	1	2	3	4	5
3	I've had energy to spare	0	1	2	3	4	5
4	I've been dealing with problems well	0	1	2	3	4	5
5	I've been thinking clearly	0	1	2	3	4	5
6	I've been feeling good about myself	0	1	2	3	4	5
7	I've been feeling close to other people	0	1	2	3	4	5
8	I've been able to make up my own mind about things	0	1	2	3	4	5
9	I've been feeling loved	0	1	2	3	4	5
10	I've been interested in new things	0	1	2	3	4	5
11	I felt inspired and motivated	0	1	2	3	4	5
12	I felt cheerful	0	1	2	3	4	5
13	I felt confident	0	1	2	3	4	5
14	I felt enthusiastic	0	1	2	3	4	5
15	I felt contentment	0	1	2	3	4	5
16	I felt that the conditions of my life are excellent	0	1	2	3	4	5
17	I felt that I am satisfied with my life	0	1	2	3	4	5
18	I felt that if I could live my life over, I would change almost nothing	0	1	2	3	4	5
19	I felt that life is good	0	1	2	3	4	5
20	I was really happy	0	1	2	3	4	5
	Sum of the above scores: Total Score for Section A =						

Happy 100 Index

Section B

Please read each statement and circle a number 0, 1, 2, 3, 4, 5 which indicates how much the statement applied to you *over the past week including today*. There are no right or wrong answers. Do not spend too much time on any statement. To get an accurate result you must answer each question honestly. Read each question carefully.

The rating scale is as follows:
0 Strongly Disagree: This did not apply to me at all
   (Not at all)
1 Disagree
2 Slightly Disagree
3 Slightly Agree
4 Agree
5 Strongly Agree: This applied to me very much
   (nearly all the time)

		Not at all					Nearly all the time
1	I felt angry	0	1	2	3	4	5
2	I felt downhearted or sad	0	1	2	3	4	5
3	I found myself getting frustrated	0	1	2	3	4	5
4	I felt lonely or remote from other people	0	1	2	3	4	5
5	I felt dissatisfied or unhappy with myself	0	1	2	3	4	5
6	I was aware of dryness of my mouth	0	1	2	3	4	5
7	I found it difficult to work up the initiative to do things	0	1	2	3	4	5
8	I tended to over-react to situations	0	1	2	3	4	5
9	I experienced trembling (e.g., in the hands)	0	1	2	3	4	5
10	I felt that I was using a lot of nervous energy	0	1	2	3	4	5
11	I was worried about situations in which I might panic and make a fool of myself	0	1	2	3	4	5
12	I felt that I had nothing to look forward to	0	1	2	3	4	5
13	I found myself getting agitated	0	1	2	3	4	5
14	I found it difficult to relax	0	1	2	3	4	5
15	I was intolerant of anything that kept me from getting on with what I was doing	0	1	2	3	4	5
16	I felt I was close to panic	0	1	2	3	4	5
17	I was unable to become enthusiastic about anything	0	1	2	3	4	5
18	I felt I wasn't worth much as a person	0	1	2	3	4	5
19	I felt scared without any good reason	0	1	2	3	4	5
20	I felt that life was meaningless	0	1	2	3	4	5
	Sum of the above scores: Total Score for Section B =						

The Happy 100 Index is a composite measure of mental health, subjective well-being and psychological well-being. It comprises the Depression, Anxiety and Stress Scales (DASS),[5] the Warwick–Edinburgh Mental Well-being Scale,[6] the Satisfaction with Life Scale[7] and a Positive and Negative Affect Balance Scale.[8]

How to calculate your Happy 100 Index score

To calculate your total Happy 100 Index score complete the questionnaire's Section A and Section B. Then simply add all your scores for Section A and divide that number by 2. This will give you subscore A. Then add all your scores for Section B and divide that number by 2. This will give you subscore B.

Now subtract subscore B from subscore A. This subtotal might be a negative number or a positive number. Make sure you keep the negative or positive sign (− or +) in front of the subtotal. Add 50 to the subtotal. If your subtotal is a negative number (−) you *subtract* the subtotal from 50 to get your final Happy 100 Index Score. If your subtotal is a positive number (+) you simply *add* 50 to your subtotal (see the table below).

Total score for Section A / divided by 2 Sub-score A	Minus	Total score for Section B / divided by 2 Sub-score B	Subtotal + or −	Add 50 to your subtotal to get your Total Happy 100 Index Score	Total Happy 100 Index Score

Here are some examples:

- Fred has a section A total score of 40 and a section B score of 70. He then divides section A score by 2 (40 / 2 = 20) and divides his section B score by 2 (70 / 2 = 35). Fred now calculates 'subscore A *minus* subscore B'; that is, 20 − 35 = −15. Finally Fred calculates 50 − 15 = 35. His Happy 100 Index score is 35.

- Jane has a section A total score of 76 and a section B score of 30. She then divides section A score by 2 (76 / 2 = 38) and divides her Section B score by 2 (30 / 2 = 15). Jane now calculates 'subscore A *minus* subscore B'; that is, 38 − 15 = + 23. Finally Jane calculates 50 + 23 = 73. Her Happy 100 Index score is 73.

Remember. You can take the Happy 100 Index once a week or every few days. We recommend that you keep a note of your score. This is designed to help you understand yourself better. To increase insight. There are no judges, no contests and this is not a competition. Use the score to keep yourself on track.

Once you have your Happy 100 score, you are ready to embark on the Eight Steps to Happiness program.

Step 1: Goals and values

Most of us take time to plan our holidays. At the least, we think about where we'd like to go, how much money we can afford to spend, how much time we can take off work, how we can fit the holiday into the children's school break. We think about what clothes we need to take, whether or not we need visas if we go overseas. We think about how the family pets will be taken care of. We buy travel insurance. We start to plan.

As we do this we start to develop a mental picture of our holiday, about what we are going to do when we get there. In our mind's eye we plan our holiday. In a way we are enjoying it even before we have got there. As we sort out the preparations and arrangements for the holiday we might find ourselves becoming frustrated. The mental picture we have developed about our holiday acts as a internal guide for us in preparing ourselves for the journey. The ideas we have about our holiday stimulate us and keep us motivated and on track. In Positive Psychology terms this is about developing 'pathways thinking',[1] thinking that keeps us moving forward towards something that we value. Not surprisingly, this is strongly related to hope and successful positive change.

Strange, isn't it, that with holidays we take all that time and trouble to plan things, yet we rarely do that with our lives. So, in a sense, we are going to do just that now, right at the beginning of this journey. In the words of Stephen Covey, we're going to start with the end in mind.[2]

As we start on this journey, the journey to fulfilling your happiness potential, the journey to a more fulfilling and meaningful life, it might be useful to develop an internal guide, a compass, a means to help us stay on track.

We are going to spend some time writing your own eulogy, a legacy letter. A eulogy is a formal speech that is a celebration of someone's life. It praises their finer qualities and highlights their achievements. Thinking about your own legacy, and writing about it, is a challenging task but a very practical one that will help you identify your core values.[3]

Why a eulogy?

The thing to remember about values is that they really keep us on track for our goals. If we don't spend time consciously identifying our values, it often becomes very hard for us to make purposeful positive change in our lives. It's like trying to travel without a compass or without signposts to show the direction forward. It's easy to get lost. We forget about the reasons we need to change. We forget about our better intentions. We get trapped in the detail of our lives and fail to see the bigger picture. Values are our guidance system, our GPS. They are the frameworks and beliefs that give us direction. In a sense they are the compass heading to which we set our lives and, by making it very clear to ourselves what those values are, they become our own personal GPS. Once we have that compass heading we can say to ourselves, 'This is the direction I want to be heading in.' But values are more than just goals. They tell us *why* we want to move in a specific direction.

When people do this exercise it often becomes really clear to them where they are right now, and where they don't want to be and why they are there. From that position we can start to really think about where we want to be and what needs to change.

Starting by thinking about the values that we are living in our lives—and the values that we're not living in our lives (and we are all doing that to some extent), is very important. But people often become very confused about what values are. In fact some people have quite a strong negative reaction to the very idea of values. They mistake values and values-based living for socially desirable behaviour or politically correct beliefs. This is not what we mean. We would rather think of values as being 'Life Principles'[4]—principles that can guide us in creating purposeful positive change in our journey towards a more fulfilling and meaningful life.

Values are similar to goals. Whereas goals are often quite specific concrete descriptions of things we would like to achieve, values are more conceptual. To 'go to the gym three times a week' is quite a specific goal. To 'be fit, active and healthy' is a value. So the difference between values and goals is that values are really higher-order or more abstract goals.

This is a list of general values. Some of these might be important to you. Perhaps all of them. Perhaps you have other values that you would need to add.

- accomplishment
- accuracy
- adventure
- altruism
- authenticity
- collaboration
- community
- comradeship
- courage
- creativity
- doing good
- empowerment
- excellence
- focus
- forgiveness
- freedom to choose
- giving
- growth
- harmony
- health
- honesty
- humour
- independence
- integrity
- interdependence
- joy
- justice
- love
- nurturing
- order
- participation
- peace
- personal power
- recognition
- respect
- reward
- self-actualisation
- spirituality
- success
- zest

You might want to make this general list of values more specific and more personal. For example, some people might have Physical Health as an important personal value. Others might see Social Justice as an important life principle. Others will aspire to 'Being a Good Father'.

Authentic values bring freedom of choice

Values

The research shows that people who pursue self-concordant goals—goals linked to their underlying interests and values—show higher subjective well-being and greater goal attainment. They also tend to experience greater goal satisfaction: they feel more satisfied when they actually reach their goals. In one study students with self-concordant motivations better attained their first-semester goals, which in turn predicted increased adjustment and greater self-concordance for the next semester's goals.[*] Interestingly, increased self-concordance in turn predicted even better goal attainment during the second semester, which led to further increases in adjustment and to higher levels of personal development by the end of the year.

[*] Sheldon, K. M. & Houser-Marko, L. (2001), 'Self-concordance, goal attainment, and the pursuit of happiness: Can there be an upward spiral?', *Journal of Personality and Social Psychology*, vol. 80, no. 1, pp. 152–65.

Knowing what your values are gives you great freedom. At the very least it means you can stop wasting time on activities that don't mean that much to you and instead spend time on things you really do care about.

We need to distinguish between the values we think that we 'ought' to have or we 'should' have, and authentic values that are really our own. So often we find ourselves doing things because we 'ought' to or because it is what other people want for us. Over time we might even become confused about how we really feel about things. We take on other people's values and beliefs. Without thinking about it, other people's values become the dominant force in our lives. We lose our authentic values, our authentic sense of self.

Some of the signs of this loss of authenticity are that we feel controlled and dominated. When we think about our values and goals we might use words like 'should', 'ought' and 'must'. Guilt, shame and anxiety characterise our thinking. The thought of failure involves panic. These are often signs that our values are 'externally controlled'—that is, these values come from other people's ideas about right and wrong—rather than our own authentic personal beliefs.

We will all have had the experience of working really hard to achieve some goal, only to find that when we got there the victory was hollow. The achievement did not really satisfy us. It was an empty victory. We might have felt like a fraud, an imposter. It was almost as if the victory belonged to someone else. We found that we did not really want it. It was not authentic, not self-concordant.

Self-concordance is when people feel that they pursue their goals because the goals fit with their real core interests and personal values, rather than because others say they should pursue them. Self-concordant goals are authentic. They feel as if they are a natural fit. When we think about them we feel energised. When we focus on them our goals and action steps become more meaningful. Mundane tasks become significant steps in the journey.

Goal-setting

Goal-setting research is extensive. Edwin Locke at the University of Maryland reviewed more than thirty years of research into the relationship between goal-setting and performance. More than 40 000 people took part in these studies, from children to nuclear research scientists, in eight different countries around the world. He concluded that specific or challenging goals resulted in better performance than easy goals or not having any goals at all.[*] The study found that, with sufficient ability and commitment, there is a direct relationship between goals and difficulty, and that the most difficult of goals produced the highest level of effort.[†] Goal-setting is most effective when there is feedback on progress to the goal, and setting goals stimulates and improves planning.

These goal-setting outcomes even cross cultures, with similar results being found in the United Kingdom, Australia, the United States, Canada, Japan, Israel and Germany.

[*] Locke, E.A., 'Motivation through conscious goal setting', *Applied and Preventive Psychology*, vol. 5, no. 2, 1996, pp. 117–24.

[†] Locke, E.A. & Latham, G.P., 'Building a practically useful theory of goal setting and ask motivation—a 35-year odyssey', *American Psychologist*, vol. 57, no. 9, 2002, pp. 705–17.

Authentic values are more than just feeling good about what we do. They increase our sense of autonomy[5]—our ability to make well-informed, purposeful choices. They also have a very real positive influence on our performance. People who set self-concordant goals are more likely to put in more effort, more likely to reach their goals[6] and more likely to feel greater overall goal satisfaction.[7] And this is not just in Western cultures. Even in cultures that emphasise people's duty to conform to societal expectations and group-centred norms such as China and South Korea, goal self-concordance—feeling that one's goals are consistent with the self—is related to happiness.[8]

Avoiding Deferred Happiness Syndrome

Identifying our authentic values and having a clear idea about the direction we want to be travelling in will help us avoid Deferred Happiness Syndrome,[9] which is the tendency to endure an unsatisfying daily life, to sacrifice one's happiness in the present, in the hope that this sacrifice will one day pay off in the long term. Of course we all need to learn to delay gratification, to put effort into reaching our goals. Deferred Happiness Syndrome comes about when this becomes a dysfunctional approach to life. We endure long hours in unsatisfying jobs. We make major sacrifices in the quality of our relationships with family and friends. We put off the thing we 'have always wanted to do'. We endure many years of stress. We endure ill-health and depression.

The motivations for deferring happiness are varied: growing aspirations for more expensive lifestyles, the need to accumulate as much as possible—particularly for one's retirement, fear of 'falling behind' one's peers and friends. Professional males especially seem to be wracked by guilt about neglecting their children while they are working long unsociable hours.

Many people live their lives thinking 'I'll be happy when …', 'I'll be happy when I drive that fancy car', 'I'll be happy when I'm 10 kilos lighter', 'I'll be happy when I'm $100 000 richer', 'I'll be happy when I'm married', 'I'll be happy when I have children' … and suddenly they are 80 and find that they forgot to be happy in all of the present moments when they could have been happy. They lose sight of their authentic values and get trapped on the treadmill of illusionary happiness.

The challenge for all of us is to break through the illusion of chasing these conditional goals—the 'I'll be happy when'—to stop living under the delusion that when we acquired that thing or gained that experience that happiness would last. But it doesn't. We become disillusioned and disappointed.

The very real danger is that we get to 80 years old and, having lived a life of conditional goals—of deferred happiness—and having missed so many opportunities for present happiness, we feel we have wasted our life. At the end of your life do you want to think back on all the opportunities when you could have derived much more contentment than you did? The thought is scary. The challenge is to take a solid look now. To see how we could be happy in the present moment. To take stock. To write our own eulogy. To start with the end in mind.

Writing your eulogy

In writing a eulogy, imagine you've lived your life, and are now—sadly—at your own funeral.

Allow yourself to get in touch with what it feels like to be there. Imagine yourself standing at the back where no one can see you but you can see and hear everything. Close your eyes and put yourself in that place. To get into the mood, you might like to imagine you can hear their voices, see their faces, get a sense of the colours or the warmth or the coldness of the place. Take your mind there—imagine.

You're listening to what people are saying—the good stuff and the not so good, the dreams, the aspirations, the things that you were connected to, the things that meant a lot to you. Perhaps it includes the things that you didn't get to do, or key opportunities that were lost. And you're standing there, listening as people talk about you. What would they say?

Take at least fifteen minutes to write your eulogy. Be honest. What are the core values and the achievements for which you would like to be remembered? Go back to the list of general values if you need prompting.

Initially Stephen found it hard to write his eulogy. But it did get him thinking. 'The process for me didn't translate readily into writing words down on a page, but it triggered an emotional response that lead me to talk to the people that are closest to me in a very direct and honest way.'

When he got home that night he took his wife and his children aside individually and told them how much he loved and valued them. 'It's the sort of thing you may think but you don't do often enough. It was very meaningful for all of us.' Later he wrote about his values in his journal:

> Honesty: I think it is important to be honest with yourself and those you encounter in your life.
> Respect/Compassion: being respectful of and compassionate towards others and being aware of the effect my actions may have in relation to others.
> Integrity: Having integrity is important. This may include being consistent, reliable and standing by your beliefs. Sometimes this may require being forthright.

When it came to writing her eulogy, Liz was stumped.

> Liz was a wonderful mother [she wrote] and couldn't think of anything more important than bringing up her children to

be respectful, well rounded, happy people. Sometimes she worried a little too much about other people's happiness and not enough about her own, but that is what made her who she was. Liz did a wonderful job in this life and has left behind people who will miss her dearly.

'That's it,' she said.

Later on she owned up to feeling enormously sad that she couldn't think of anything, other than her parenting, for which her peers would remember her. 'I drew a blank. I couldn't think of anything that people would be saying about me.'

The eulogy exercise was a catalyst for Liz. It spurred her to think long and hard about her goals and her values. Although she rightly valued being a good mother, she had not really defined her life in terms of who she wanted to be. She was putting her life on hold, hanging out for a better future, yet one she could not as yet envisage. She hadn't written herself into the picture of her life.

With Dr Tony's help she came to see that she was sacrificing her own self-esteem by playing her life roles in accordance with other people's wishes—not her own. In her journal she wrote, 'Learn to like yourself for who you are and how happy you can be while being yourself, not how happy you can make others.'

He encouraged her to start being more authentic in her choices, to pay less attention to what she thought she should be doing, and more attention to what felt authentic and genuine to her.

When you are living by your goals and values, often what feels like something you should do can become something you choose to do and derive pleasure from. For example, sitting down with the kids to do their homework can feel like a chore—something you should do. But when you take the emphasis off it being something you *should* do, and think about it as being something you *choose* to do, it becomes more like something you *want* to do. By changing our thinking, by purposefully focusing on our values and goals, we can change the meaning we give to events, making our experience more rewarding—happier.

Liz embraced that notion. 'That is something that I'd like, that I know I can learn to enjoy. It's a chore, because I'm time poor. I'm trying to squeeze in too much and I'm losing the joy from things. I need to look at that differently. I'm doing that as a service to my kids. They're going to grow up to be better educated. I have to think about the bigger picture.'

When it came to writing his eulogy, Ben did something quite unusual. He wrote two. The first represented the real story as he saw it if he were to die tomorrow:

> There's a small congregation of people in a sunny, breezy place not far from the sea, a couple of friends, maybe Baz and Gabi speak of my unwavering desire to have fun and to lighten the mood. Mum speaks of my unfulfilled ambition to travel and experience the world … Some speak of my willingness to help out to the best of my ability, when somebody needs it, but there's also disappointment that I was unable to do the things that I wanted to do in my life … a sense that I procrastinated too much about deciding what to do with my life and taking actions … Everybody wishes I had taken more chances and realised more opportunities. That's pretty accurate, if I was to have a funeral tomorrow.

The second was very different:

> Gabi speaks of my adventures through South-East Asia and Europe and tells tales of exploring pristine beaches and beautiful remote locations, bustling cities, crowded laneways, multitudes of cuisine and culture … Mum speaks of my willingness to help out whenever help is needed and always being caring and loyal … Some tell of my volunteer work with less fortunate people in Australia and abroad. Evan and Dana speak of my

travelling as much as I can throughout Australia, my many adventures in quiet towns, in the Outback and the tropics. All speak of my desire to have fun and keep the mood light.

Doing this exercise helped Ben to realise that he had lost his authentic sense of self. His lifestyle revolved around issues of financial security and creature comforts. He was making safe choices on the basis of what he thought he should do, yet he felt stifled by the security he was clinging to. He confessed to being sick of being stuck in a rut and resolved to 'grab the bull by the horns'.

Before you write

Some final thoughts before you write. What this exercise is about is exploring how we see our lives now and how we see the values that we're living our lives by or not living our lives by. So it's not about: 'Did I write the best eulogy?' It is much more about: what was my experience of writing that?

It is important to remember that we never really completely fulfil our values. In a sense they're almost like a direction—heading east or heading west. You can move in that direction but you never get there—you never get to 'east' or 'west'. What is important as you move on this journey is that you know what the next stop is, you know what the next goal is, the next action that you're going to take that's going to move you in the right direction towards fulfilling your own personal potential.

As the eulogies from the *Making Australia Happy* program show, there's no single way to address this exercise. Try to be true to your feelings and instincts and not start rationalising how you think it ought to read.

Allow yourself to really get in touch with the process. Put as much effort into this as if you were going on a $5000 holiday. After all, it is your life.

After you write

There are three key things to do after you write your eulogy. These three things are designed to turn insight into action.

First, reflect on your experience of doing the eulogy. Ask yourself what you learnt from writing it. These insights can take place on a number of different levels. It could be, 'Oh, I need to pay more attention to this or that aspect of my life.' But equally it could be that 'I find it very difficult for me to stand back and reflect on who I am'. Another type of learning might be about how you live your life, or it could be about how you think about your life.

Whatever your learning, spend some time writing it down in a journal. Journalling and diary-keeping have been shown by numerous studies to have a really positive influence and to provide a framework for reflection.

Next, consider whether the values you listed are really yours and not someone else's, not your parents', or the externally controlled 'shoulds'. Sit with the values you identify. Spend some time thinking about them and ask yourself: do they feel comfortable? Do they feel like they're yours, or do they feel like they're someone else's? Settle on the values that feel most real to you.

Finally, reflection on its own isn't enough. We need to move from insight to action. So the third thing is to identify two or three little things that you can do to help move you forward towards creating purposeful positive change. For some people these might be really small things, like coming home from work early, or doing more—or even less—around the house. For others it might be about spending more time on your own. What ever those action steps are, write them down, make sure they reflect your authentic values and do them!

Step 2: Random acts of kindness

As you weave though the rush-hour traffic, anxious and upset because you are late for work, you notice the bumper sticker on the car in front of you: 'Warning: I perform random acts of kindness.' Stressed and impatient, your inner cynic responds, 'Do us all a favour—just stop the random driving'—or maybe, 'I'll give you acts of kindness … get your random butt out of my way.' The more pragmatic cynic might think, 'Why are cars with those stickers always so rundown? Are they hoping someone will be kind to them when they break down?' Most of us can indentify with at least one of these cynical voices.

Even the non-cynic might wonder how many people would actually find the bumper sticker inspiring. How many would be motivated to actually do some random act of kindness, and, even if they did, would it really make any difference? After all, we reason, the notion of random kindness is more New Age than solid contemporary science.

Sitting in your car as you follow this train of thought, you might also find yourself reflecting on whether or not you are a kind person yourself. Do you pass on good things to others? Do you? Of course, we all give sometimes—but do we do it without preconditions?

So, right now take a minute to think about some of the acts of unconditional kindness you have done for others or that others have done for you. Right now, pause and think about the good things that came out of that. Think about how you felt. How they might have felt. Chances are that this memory evokes pleasant thoughts, maybe even strong ones, good feelings, a warm glow.

As a result of this mental experiment you might feel like doing some small act of kindness for someone else. You might even make a mental note resolving to do so in the near future. You've probably made this kind of resolution in the past too.

But of course life goes on. We become busy. We become stressed. We forget. We fail to notice the opportunities to make a small positive difference in someone else's life. We return to our own needs. Taking care of business. Keeping ourselves buoyant in troubled times. Altruism becomes the last thing on our minds.

What is altruism? Altruism has been defined as a motivational state with the ultimate goal of increasing another's welfare, an unselfish regard for or devotion to the welfare of others.[1] It is linked to giving, volunteering and performing acts of service to others. It is the opposite of egoism, selfishness and hostility.

The notion of altruism is central to all the major religions. Compassion, caring and doing good for others sits at the core of the Buddhist philosophy. Christians are exalted to 'love your neighbour as you do yourself'. Mohammed proclaimed that Moslems should 'wish for their brother what they wish for themselves'. The Sufi religion teaches that one should give preference to others rather than oneself when doing a good deed, giving precedence to the common interests of the community over one's own interests. Judaism promotes the idea that people cannot be truly righteous if they don't demonstrate an unselfish concern for others.

Although the concepts related to altruism are longstanding within religious traditions, it was only in the nineteenth century that the term *altruism* itself was coined by the French philosopher Auguste Comte (1798–1857). Deriving from the Latin *alter hic* ('this other') the term *altruism* was used to designate conduct impelled by motives that were utterly unselfish and were inspired by a desire to bring about the happiness or well-being of another without regard to the cost to oneself or even at one's own expense.

What motivates altruism?

Can we ever be truly purely altruistic, or are all acts of altruism really self-serving in some way? One side of this interesting philosophical debate argues that pure altruism is a completely selfless act that intentionally benefits another, incurs no direct personal benefit whatsoever and sometimes even bears a personal cost.[2] Another side of the debate argues that such pure altruism cannot exist because supposedly pure altruistic acts always benefit the giver in some way. The benefits might range from a pleasurable feeling, a warm glow,[3] social acceptance through adherence to social norms such as reciprocity or perceived generosity leading to increased personal status within a society or community,[4] or even the survival of a whole species.

Although these are interesting philosophical discussion points, our focus in this book is on pragmatics—what works in practice. If we are to practise altruism we need to be clear about when we are being really altruistic and when we are primarily being self-serving. We need a way to distinguish between self-serving altruism[5] and what we are calling other-centred altruism.

Self-serving altruism are acts that look apparently altruistic from the outside but are primarily inspired or motivated by people's own self-interest. These are acts of altruism that are done primarily (for example) to make us look good, to boost our status, to make use feel superior. In contrast, other-centred acts of altruism are motivated primarily by the desire to benefit the other person, and that this is the overwhelming motive, regardless of whether or not the giver receives some ancillary benefit from the act. In our quest to understand happiness and the application of coaching and positive psychology to our lives, the distinction between self-serving altruism and other-centred altruism can act as a useful guideline to help us determine whether an act is really altruistic.

So, what is the relationship between altruism and happiness?

Paying tax can feel good

Even paying tax can make the donor happier, according to a 2007 study from the University of Oregon,[*] if it is seen to be in the public good.

A group of female students was recruited to play a 'giving to charity' game. Each was issued with $100 cash and told that they could keep whatever was left at the end of the game. They were also told about a local food bank that would benefit from any donations from their account. The game required the students to interact with a screen as the computer set up a series of transactions in and out of their accounts. While they played, their brains were scanned by a functional magnetic resonance (fMRI) machine.

Sometimes the computer offered the students the opportunity to donate to the food bank. Sometimes it automatically 'taxed' the account by transferring money to the food bank without their approval. Occasionally extra money from an unknown source would appear either in the student's account or in the food bank account.

When most students chose to make a donation the reward centres of their brains lit up—the same areas that respond to pleasurable things like chocolate, sex or receiving money. Given that altruism has been shown to increase happiness levels, this was not unexpected. It's the 'warm glow effect'.

The surprising feature was that some of the students showed signs of what is called 'pure altruism'. When they saw money appear in the food account as a result of an automatic transfer from their own account, their pleasure centres still lit up, although not as much as when they had been instrumental in giving. Even more surprising, they reacted more positively to seeing the extra money arrive in the food bank than in their own account.

The co-author of the study, Ulrich Mayr, feels that these findings have implications for fiscal policies as they indicate that some people care more about money going to the public good than to themselves.

Overall, the study established that both seeing a charity receive money and giving money to charity activates the same areas of the brain, but that the warm glow effect from free choice promotes the bigger response.

[*] Harbaugh, W.T., Mayr, U. & Burghart, D.R., 'Neural responses to taxation and voluntary giving reveal motives for charitable donations', *Science*, vol. 316, 2007, pp. 162–5.

Happy people are more altruistic

There is good evidence to show that happy people are more helpful, give more to charities and other worthy causes and are generally more altruistic.

The research on how positive moods are related to altruistic behaviour goes back a long way. Research in the 1970s found that people who were in a good mood after they found a coin in the coin return of a public telephone while they were making a phone call, or by unexpectedly receiving cookies, were more likely to be spontaneously helpful (for example) by helping to pick up things that had been accidentally dropped by someone else.[6] But good moods do more than just encourage altruistic behaviour. One study found that people in a good mood also tended to seek out more information— they were more inquisitive as well as helpful.[7]

Charities can also benefit from happiness. In one experiment college students who were happy volunteered to help in charity collections far more than those in a neutral or negative mood.[8] Happiness also translates into increased financial donations to charities, and the effect is particularly strong when people are reminded about their own personal goals for self-improvement.[9]

And it seems that giving is better than receiving. A ground-breaking large-scale study of 2016 church members found that helping others was associated with higher levels of mental health, well above and beyond the benefits of receiving help.[10]

Happiness and altruism are also linked in the workplace. One 2009 American study closely followed eight people over a working week, getting them to complete five surveys each day using a Palm Pilot.[11] The participants were randomly contacted over the course of the day, and then they had to enter information about their mood and a number of experiences, including whether they had helped someone since the previous survey. This study allowed the researchers to study the effect of positive moods on altruism and helping behaviour over time. They found an important link between positive moods, helping behaviour and the personality trait of altruism. It is important to remember that individuals naturally vary in their basic predisposition to altruism—some people are naturally helpful. Unfortunately others are not. The study found that, when they were feeling very happy, the naturally unhelpful people became just as altruistic as those who were naturally very helpful. High levels of happiness seemed to make everyone more altruistic—even the 'difficult' people!

What's more, the link between positive moods and altruism seems to be cross-cultural and has a positive impact on work performance as well as general helping behaviour. One Taiwanese study collected data from 588 insurance sales agents and found that positive moods predicted task performance both through interpersonal factors (for example, helping and supporting coworkers) and through increased motivational processes, such as self-confidence and task persistence.[12]

So altruism is useful at work. But what about holidays? Imagining that you are on holiday can also increase altruism! In one study researchers induced happiness by asking people to imagine themselves on a beautiful Hawaiian vacation.[13] Following this imaginary holiday the participants were more helpful to the researcher (by filling out more questionnaires) than a control group who did not take the imaginary vacation.

Does altruism cause happiness?

The idea that happy people are more altruistic makes good intuitive sense and, as we have seen, research over many years shows that. But the real question is: do acts of altruism increase happiness and well-being? Does altruism cause happiness?

This is a difficult question to study because it is not easy to tease out the different factors that are specially related to increases in happiness. One way to do this is to conduct an experiment and give money to people to spend either on themselves or on others. People in one such study were given either five or twenty dollars, then randomly assigned to spending this windfall on a bill, expense or a gift for themselves, or to spend the money on a gift for someone else or a donation to a charity.[14] Those who spent the money on other people or gave it to a charity were happier at the end of the day than those who spent the money on themselves. What's more, the amount of money they spent (five or twenty dollars) did not influence their happiness levels at the end of the day—which suggests that is it how people spend their money that counts, not the amount spent. It seems that even relatively small altruistic donations can increase our levels of well-being.

Another good way to explore the influence of altruism on happiness and well-being is to study how people change over a long period. Longitudinal studies can give us insights about the real world in a way that is difficult in experiments. One study followed 427 wives and mothers from upstate New York for thirty years and found that those women who did volunteer work at least once a week lived longer and had better physical functioning, even after accounting for number of children, occupation, education and other factors, such as social class.[15]

The link between altruism and long-term health and happiness is fairly well established. The good news is that altruism can have life-long benefits. A study that started in California in the 1930s and interviewed a group of adolescents every ten years until the late 1990s found that adolescents who engaged in altruistic pro-social behaviour such as helping others when they were young had better mental and physical health in adulthood.[16] Surprisingly, the positive effects of altruism were not related to social class or how religious the person was. It seemed from the study that the key factors were emotions such as givingness and warmth, and the researchers suggested that it was the ability to put emotions of that kind into practice through acts of altruism that made the real long-term difference.

So we know that altruism and acts of kindness and giving increase levels of happiness and well-being and even make you live longer.

The question is: how much is enough? How much do we need to do for others before we ourselves get the positive effects? The answer could be about two hours per week. A large-scale longitudinal study of 4860 elderly people, which looked at the effects of doing volunteer and paid work in old age, found strong positive effects on well-being for those who did up to a hundred hours annually.[17] Doing more than a hundred hours annually did not increase well-being over the levels associated with a hundred hours. Of course the exact amount of weekly volunteering needed to increase happiness will vary from person to person, and because this study looked at volunteer and paid work together, we can't distinguish the exact separate effects of volunteer work alone. Nevertheless it seems as if we don't have to put too much time in each week to receive the benefits, and even volunteering on a random one-off basis will have immediate effects on our well-being.

With this in mind, *Making Australia Happy* arranged for our eight participants to help out for a couple of hours at the Exodus Foundation. The Exodus Foundation draws on an army of around a thousand volunteers to provide food, healthcare and education to the homeless and the disadvantaged. According to Reverend Bill Crews, who runs the charity, volunteers and donors alike tell him that working there or giving money makes them feel good, and the more they give, the better they feel.

Anyone in need can get a free meal at the charity's restaurant every day from Monday to Saturday, and hundreds do. Some of the *Making Australia Happy* team helped in the kitchen while others waited on tables. Liz and Tony, who are naturally sociable, spent a lot of time talking to the clientele. Others, like Cade, preferred to keep a low profile, clearing plates and wiping tables. He was initially quite anxious about interacting with so many people he had never met before, but he was extremely grateful for the experience.

'Once we got into it I actually really, really enjoyed it. I've always secretly thought of doing something like this, but I've never had the guts to actually go through with it … it's a pocket of society that you're aware of, but unless it's right in front of your face, you forget about it, because life's so hectic. So being told you can actually assist and help out on this very small scale, it's instant gratification. I probably felt the happiest I've felt during this whole entire program.'

Stephen found the experience so inspiring that he determined to make more time for helping out in his immediate community. 'The thing about altruism is that you do get a reward and it does enrich what you're doing. With four kids there is always a lot of opportunities to get involved at a level that really relates to them too, the sporting teams and so on, so I guess that is where I see my focus.'

Every single one of them found it to be a rewarding experience, and the proof was in the pudding, or rather in their saliva. We took samples of everybody's saliva before and after the volunteering session. We were expecting to see an increase in immunoglobulin antibodies, which protect the body from common illnesses like colds and flu. Our experiment worked! Sure enough, we saw a boost of about 35 per cent, more than a third, a significant result and from just two hours of volunteering.

Can altruism ever be harmful?

Altruism can cause harm under some circumstances. Occupational altruism is central to many professions such as medicine, counselling or social work. When these are associated with high levels of stress, low levels of resources and overwhelming demands, the result can be empathy fatigue[18] or professional burnout. Altruistic individuals who are primary caregivers to family members with chronic debilitating disorders, such as dementia, might also experience significant negative effects on their own health if they have insufficient support or respite.

Some altruistic individuals are so focused on helping others that they become neglectful of their own self-care, and can end up leading impoverished, grey and joyless lives. Some of them even have great difficulty in recognising and in meeting their own basic needs. However, a selfless or other-centred approach to helping others is not the same as destroying or sacrificing oneself. We suggest that this kind of dysfunctional altruism is best avoided.

It is important to realise that we need to take care of ourselves if we are to be able to truly give to others. This might sound selfish or egotistical, but it's not. Take care of yourself so that you can take care of others. Renewal, regeneration, revitalisation are the foundations of sustainable altruism.

The trap of purposefully giving to feel better

The paradox of all this is that, while the research shows that altruistic behaviour does indeed increase happiness and well-being, if we act altruistically specifically in order to feel better, we might end up feeling worse! At the least, we might not feel as good as we anticipated. We might even feel anger and resentment towards those who do not appropriately express gratitude for our altruistic acts. It's easy to see how we could easily fall into a victim mindset. This mindset says, 'I do all this good work for others unasked, out of the goodness of my own heart, and no one appreciates me.'

One way to deal with this is to understand our motives for altruism. We need to check that our motivations are primarily about the other person, not ourselves. We need to place our attention firmly on them. Self-focused attention reduces our ability to be altruistic and reduces pro-social behaviour.[19] But how can we know whether our acts of altruism are for real?

The altruism litmus test

A simple way to increase the chances that our altruism is truly other-centred is to see how we feel if we are not thanked for our efforts. For example, when driving in heavy traffic, letting someone's car into the traffic ahead of us is a simple altruistic act, an everyday random act of kindness. Here's the litmus test for altruism. If you feel disturbed, upset or angry after you have let their car in front of you and they do not thank you, then that act does not meet the criterion for other-centred altruism. This is because your motives, as revealed after the event, show that you were really expecting some kind of reward or acknowledgement for your behaviour. Because of that, your act can just be classified as well-mannered behaviour—good manners. Good manners are nice to have and pleasant for other people to experience. But good manners are not altruism!

Try the test yourself. It's an invaluable of-the-moment check of other-centred altruistic intention.

Practise random acts of kindness

Many of us will not be able to find the time to commit to regular volunteering work. If you can commit to regular volunteer work, that's great. But for many people life is too busy as it is—never mind taking on more commitments! But we can all experience the benefits of altruism simply by committing random acts of kindness. It's simple to do. It takes very little time. And it works. Random acts of kindness have been scientifically shown to increase happiness and well-being. Even hard-nosed lawyers have been successfully practising this exercise in law firms.[20]

What exactly is a random act of kindness? One definition says:

> a random act of kindness is a selfless act performed by a person or persons wishing to either assist or cheer up an individual or in some cases an animal. There will generally be no reason other than to make people smile, or be happier. Either spontaneous or planned in advance, random acts of kindness are often encouraged by various communities such as commercial or community organisations.[21]

We introduced our volunteers to the notion of random acts of kindness by giving each of them $20 and letting them loose in the main shopping mall in Marrickville. At first they were rather inhibited because it felt very contrived, and Ben found it confronting when his offers to carry shopping bags or push heavy trolleys were rejected. But following a conversation with Dr Tony, Ben changed his approach. He chose an older man to give money to for a coffee and cake, and ended up having up having a long conversation with him.

Liz was nervous, dreading the embarrassment of not knowing whether she was going to be rejected. Eventually she settled upon the idea of buying a bunch of flowers for someone who would really appreciate them. 'I knew I wanted to give them to a female and I wanted to give them to a mum, someone who is run off their feet ... and then I started thinking about the age group and I saw a woman around my mum's age group when she died in her seventies ... Boy, did she appreciate it! She was hugging and kissing me ... I couldn't have found anyone in that shopping centre who would have appreciated them any more than she did. I wasn't expecting that; I was expecting someone to get all flustered and say: "What's it for?" It was great. It was most emotional and it made me feel fantastic, above and beyond what I thought I would have felt.'

Of all of them, Stephen was the most surprised at how something so simple could be so enjoyable and so effective. 'I was tired after a busy day at work, and it was just not what I wanted to be involved in,' he remembered later. However, he took it on board, and came up with the idea of buying a carton of wrapped chocolates, which he offered to shoppers as they waited at the check-out. 'The responses I got from people were fantastic It gave me a lot of confidence in humankind. I was really surprised. I came from a position of "I really don't want to do this" to really getting a great benefit out of it.'

Organised kindness

Although the idea of performing spontaneous acts of kindness for others is literally ancient, it is only recently that the phrase 'random acts of kindness' entered contemporary Western culture. Since Anne Herbert reportedly coined the phrase 'Practice random acts of kindness and senseless beauty' in a Sausalito restaurant in 1982,[22] the idea of performing intentional random acts of kindness in a systematic and organised way has mushroomed. Not surprisingly, the media love the idea.

Radio DJs in the United States, United Kingdom, Canada and South Africa have promoted Kindness Days. The 'Free Hugs' video on YouTube received more than 57 915 000 hits. The book *Random Acts of Kindness* was released by Conari Press in 1993. A non-profit organisation, the Random Acts of Kindness Foundation, was established in 1995. The movie *Pay It Forward*, released in 2000, was based on a book called *Pay It Forward*, by Catherine Ryan Hyde, which itself was inspired by the notion of random acts of kindness. The One Million Random Acts of Kindness Campaign was launched on BBC Radio in 2008.

There are many kindness organisations worldwide. One UK organisation, the Kindness Offensive (TKO) runs large-scale random acts of kindness for the public. Its Kindness Events include giving away 25 tonnes of food, giving hundreds of free tickets to see West End musicals, concerts, sporting events, and even musical instruments, kitchen equipment and electrical goods! On Pancake Day, 24 February 2009, TKO gave away 500 000 pancakes, most of them to charities.[23]

So there is quite a substantial random acts of kindness movement worldwide. But what about the science? Does it work?

Random acts of kindness: the science

A number of studies have looked at the effect of committing random acts of kindness. In the best known study to date, college students were asked to perform five random acts of kindness in one day each week over the course of six weeks.[24] These acts of kindness were described as acts that benefited others or made others happy, typically at some cost to the giver. Examples included putting coins into a stranger's parking meter, donating blood, helping someone with a problem or visiting someone who was sick. The results were quite impressive. While the control group experienced a reduction in happiness over the six-week period, the random acts of kindness group experienced an increase. The data shows that there was no difference between the two groups at the beginning of the six weeks, but the random acts of kindness group had a 41.66 per cent increase in well-being compared to the control group after six weeks. It works!

So, how can we benefit from this research? The instructions given to the people in the study provide very useful guidelines. This is what they were told:[25]

In our daily lives, we all perform acts of kindness for others. These acts may be large or small and the person for whom the act is performed may or may not be aware of the act. Examples include feeding a stranger's parking meter, donating blood, helping a friend with homework, visiting an elderly relative, or writing a thank you letter. One day each week, you are to perform five acts of kindness. The acts do not need to be for the same person, the person may or may not be aware of the act, and the act may or may not be similar to the acts listed above. Do not perform any acts that may place yourself or others in danger.

Our volunteers became quite creative with their random acts of kindness. Here is a 'random' list of some of the things they did:

- Liz K swept the leaves from her neighbour's garden path and emptied another neighbour's bins.
- Stephen gave a box of fruit he put together from a trip to the Flemington produce markets to a local boarding house for the mentally ill, and took a homebrew beer over to his neighbour on a Friday afternoon.
- Cade gave $10 to a homeless beggar and trimmed his neighbour's hedge.
- Ben bought a coffee for a lonely old man and sat talking to him for half an hour.
- Natalia prepared a bubble bath for her flatmate.
- Liz burned a music CD for her neighbour.
- Rebekah made cold drinks for the builders working in sweltering heat on a neighbour's house.
- Tony bought a pair of new shoes for a homeless friend.

Try this exercise for yourself. One day each week perform five random acts of kindness. Here are thirty more ideas for acts of kindness to get you started:[26]

In everyday life

- In a café or restaurant leave an extra big tip for a small bill.
- Give some money or groceries to a beggar or street person.
- Let someone in front of you in the traffic or in a queue.
- Open the door for someone.
- Give someone the gift of your time—do something for someone that requires time and effort.
- Explicitly thank people for their effort or for good service.
- Say something nice to everyone you meet today.
- Pay for coffee or a movie ticket for the person behind you.
- Renew an old friendship by sending a letter or gift.
- When driving, stop to let people cross the road.

In the workplace
- Take time to show your appreciation to your co-workers or employees.
- Donate a percentage of your revenue for a day to a group in need.
- Invite someone new to lunch and pay for it.
- Help an overwhelmed co-worker with their tasks.
- Surprise someone with a snack, drink or coffee.
- Give a compliment.
- Remember others' birthdays and important events.
- Praise someone who has helped you to their boss.
- Write a thank you note to someone who went out of their way to help you.
- Give a surprise treat to your employees—take them for a meal or let them leave an hour early.

In your community
- Talk to a lonely neighbour.
- Volunteer in your community.
- Clean up a public space—pick up litter.
- Plant some flowers—create a community garden.
- Call or visit a homebound person.
- Mow a neighbour's lawn.
- Collect goods for a charity.
- Help out at a soup kitchen or homeless shelter.
- Organise a neighbourhood party.
- Mentor or teach young people in your neighbourhood.

From thinking to doing

Of course, these acts of kindness are not truly random. It's natural and important for us to think about how our acts will be received. It is also important to make sure that we do not place ourselves in any danger while performing altruistic acts. So these are not really random.

But they are intentional. To make this count we need to chose to perform these acts and do so mindfully. Paying attention to what we do. Doing it on purpose, not on autopilot. So look out for opportunities to practise intentional acts of kindness.

Take time to notice what happens when you commit these acts of kindness. Reflect on your experience. Record your actions in your journal.

Remember to avoid the trap of being superficially altruistic in order to feel better. Act primarily because it is a good thing to do. It can be really small gestures, but the hallmark is that you do it genuinely as an act of giving. Do it for others, and the personal benefits will follow.

Be careful—random acts of kindness may become addictive! Enjoy!

Step 3: Mindfulness

Most of us race through life on automatic pilot, oblivious of the present. Asleep. We are rarely truly aware of the present moment. Mindless. In contrast, mindfulness is a mental state of awareness and openness that helps people live more consciously by opening the senses and refocusing attention on the here and now. One adopts a non-evaluative and non-judgemental approach to the stream of thoughts and emotions that make up one's inner experience.

We can use mindfulness to 'wake up', connect with ourselves and appreciate the fullness of each moment of life. The practice of mindfulness reduces stress hormones and leaves the brain open to new experiences. It's a crucial element of happiness. In step 3, we learn how to engage fully in everyday experiences to deal more effectively with difficult thoughts and emotions. We'll learn to deal with more—by doing less.

In this consumer-based century we're enticed to want more, buy more, use more, consume more. Mobile phones and emails make us contactable twenty-four hours a day. We are time-poor and worry increasingly about the future. Our heads become so full of this chatter that we fail to notice or simply take for granted the good things in the here and now.

One of the most powerful ways to combat this turmoil is to cultivate mindfulness, paying attention to the world around us, instead of being caught up in our thoughts. Attuning our attention. Redirecting our attentional focus. Dr Russ Harris, the 'Mindfulness Coach' for *Making Australia Happy*, defines mindfulness as 'paying attention with openness, curiosity and flexibility'.

What is mindfulness?

Until recently in the Western world you could learn about mindfulness only through following ancient Eastern practices like meditation, yoga, tai chi, martial arts or philosophical and spiritual pathways like Buddhism, Taoism or Zen.

But in the last thirty years, mindfulness practices have become part and parcel of mainstream Western psychology. Many of these scientifically validated models teach mindfulness through traditional methods such as meditation and yoga, but others teach it in ways that are often better suited to the agenda of the twenty-first-century lifestyle.

Dr Russ Harris is one of Australia's leading practitioners of Acceptance and Commitment Therapy (ACT).[1] ACT is one of a number of cognitive behavioural therapies that place a major emphasis on developing mindfulness skills. But ACT is very user-friendly. It does not emphasise the formal practice of meditation for two simple reasons: most people are reluctant to practise formal meditation, and there are other often quicker and easier ways to learn these skills. We are going to explore these in this section.

'Mindfulness is about opening up and taking in what's going on around us. It helps us stop living in our thoughts and start living in the here and now,' says Dr Russ. 'The goal of ACT is to create a rich

Mindfulness

Mindfulness promotes structural and functional changes in the brain. In the normal course of events, the right side of the prefrontal cortex, at the front of the brain, becomes overactive when we are emotionally disturbed whereas the left prefrontal cortex is underactive. Study after study has found that after practising meditation on a regular basis, the balance starts to shift. The left prefrontal cortex, which is the part that keeps you engaged and focused and in the present moment, starts to become more active. The right prefrontal cortex, the part that gets you emotionally worked up and disturbed, starts to settle down.

In 2007 Norman Farb and his colleagues at Toronto University shed further light on how mindfulness reshapes our neural networks.[*] They began with the premise that we spend most of our lives experiencing the world through the filter of what is going on in our heads, creating a 'narrative' through which we perceive our self, with reference to the world around us. They set out to investigate what is going on in the brain when we try to ignore our internal dialogue and enjoy the 'experiential' sense of the self by paying attention in the present moment.

They were able to demonstrate that there are two distinct neural networks regulating both kinds of experience, the 'experiential ' and the 'narrative', and that whereas most people have difficulty dissociating the two networks, people with some training in mindfulness are better able to switch between the two.

They recruited people from a hospital stress clinic to participate in an eight-week training program in mindfulness. Together with a control group, they were instructed on the difference between experiencing the world through savouring current sensations and getting caught up in the mind's mental chatter.

Both groups were shown a series of emotionally evocative words like 'honest', 'loving', 'stoic' and 'cowardly' and asked to respond by deliberately thinking about the connotations of those words: 'Am I honest?' 'Do I admire courage?' 'I remember how it felt falling in love', and so on. Then they had to respond to a similar series of words paying attention only to the words on the screen. If memories or judgements surfaced they were instructed to let the thoughts come and go but not to get caught up in them. Their brains were scanned during the process.

When they were instructed to experience the words in the 'narrative' mode by thinking about them and making judgements about them, both groups showed similar brain activity in the part of the brain that deals with analysis and evaluation, the cortical midline area. When instructed simply to pay attention to the words on the screen both groups showed less activity in that same cortical midline area. But the exciting finding was that when they were in this experiential mode the group who had done mindfulness training displayed activity in a completely separate area of the brain associated with feeling sensations in the here and now, the right insula.

Farb and his colleagues had found hard neural evidence that humans can train their minds to alternate, at will, between immediate experience and conceptual thinking. 'Training the mind to pay attention to the present moment may create

>

long-term neural changes in the brains of people with mood disorders,' says Norman Farb, 'and so help lift them out of entrenched modes of thinking that keep them stuck in an unhelpful narrative that continually promotes a negative life view.'

* Farb, N.A.S., Segal, Z.V., Mayberg, H. et al., 'Attending to the present: Mindfulness meditation reveals distinct neural modes of self-reference', *Social Cognitive and Affective Neuroscience*, vol. 2, no. 4, 2007, pp. 313–22.

and meaningful life while accepting the pain that inevitably goes with it. Mindfulness enables you to reduce the influence of unhelpful thoughts and difficult feelings, and enables you to live with them while fully engaging in the present moment.'

In scientific studies, mindfulness has been associated with lasting decreases in a variety of stress-related physical symptoms, including chronic pain;[2] significant decreases in anxiety and depression;[3] improved concentration and creativity; improved immune system functioning and decreased symptoms secondary to cancer.[4] ACT in particular has been shown to be effective for social anxiety, depression, drug addiction, obsessive compulsive disorder, chronic pain syndrome, epilepsy, weight loss, quitting smoking,[5] diabetes self-management, coping with cancer, schizophrenia, work stress and performance enhancement.[6]

Negative thoughts

Our minds have evolved to think negatively, constantly throwing up difficult and challenging thoughts for us. Although we can all learn to think more positively, this will not stop our minds from coming up with negative thoughts.

Many psychological approaches suggest that negative thoughts are toxic or harmful and that you need to get rid of them. ACT suggests this is largely futile. As Dr Russ says, 'Zen masters are like the Olympic athletes of mind-training, and even they have plenty of negative thoughts. Trying to get rid of them is a waste of time and effort. Instead of fighting with our thoughts, disputing them, or trying to get rid of them, we can learn to change our relationship with them. We can take all the power out of them, so that when they show up, they don't control us. We can learn how to let them come and go without getting caught up in them. Mindfulness enables us to do this.'

Most scientists agree that our species, *Homo sapiens*, appeared on the planet about 100 000 years ago. Back then the world was a dangerous place. It was eat or be eaten; kill or be killed. The mind had to anticipate the worst, look for things that could hurt or harm us, and stop us getting wounded or killed.

Dr Russ says, 'If the mind of a caveman wasn't good at spotting or anticipating threats, he got killed pretty quickly. We didn't evolve from cavemen like that; we evolved from the ones who were always on the lookout for danger. As a result, the modern human mind is constantly trying to warn us of things that can hurt or harm us. It's no wonder we all have a tendency to worry, or predict the worst.'

The modern human mind is a double-edged sword. It's very useful for all sorts of different things, such as clarifying your values, setting goals, planning and strategising, problem-solving, communication, creativity and so on. But the dark side of the mind is that it has a tendency to be very unhelpful. As Dr Russ puts it, 'A lot of the time, our mind is like "Radio Doom and Gloom" dredging up painful memories from the past and conjuring up scary scenarios about the future. It's like a time machine, constantly pulling us into the past or drawing us into the future, and making it very hard to stay present.'

Negative thoughts and the inner critic

We're all acquainted with the inner critic—that voice in your head that is constantly nagging, telling you that whatever you are doing, you're not doing it well enough. It's also very quick to judge and criticise. Why is this?

Again, go back 100 000 years. Imagine seeing the shadow of some-one coming towards you. You quickly have to make the decision—friend or foe? Obviously it's going to be far safer to err on the defensive side; to assume it's a foe and prepare yourself. Consequently, our mind has evolved to make snap judgements, very quickly, many of which are negative.

We can logically and rationally recognise that our mind does this, but that doesn't stop it from happening; from churning out judgements like a machine on automatic: judgement after judgement after judgement. Listen to your mind for five minutes and notice how many judgements it comes up with. Try it. Sit quietly for five minutes right now and listen to your mind. What's your inner voice saying?

Dr Russ says, 'We can't stop the mind from judging, but we can learn to see that these judgements are just words popping into our head. And we can learn how to let them come and go without getting all caught up in them.'

Mindfulness helps us change our relationship with our mind. It allows us to treat the mind chatter as if it's a radio playing in the background. If it's broadcasting something helpful that we can use, we can tune in and allow it to guide our actions. But if it's just broadcasting the usual doom and gloom stuff—the judgements, the dwelling on the past, the worrying about the future—then, by practising mindfulness we can let it play on in the background while we live in the present and focus on the task at hand.

Emotions

Happiness is not the same thing as feeling good. Happiness means living a rich and full and meaningful life. The things that make life rich, full and meaningful, such as building close relationships, usually give rise to the full range of human emotions, from love and joy to fear and sadness. As with our thoughts, mindfulness can help us handle our emotions more effectively.

Think of your closest relationships with children, parents, partners, friends. In the rich tapestry of love and friendship, it won't have been entirely smooth sailing. Along with the pleasant emotions, you will also at times feel anxiety, sadness, or anger.

'Love and pain are intimate dance partners. Painful emotions are a valuable parts of a life fully lived. Imagine how difficult life would be if you were unable to experience sadness or guilt or fear; these emotions contribute to a rich and full life,' says Dr Russ. 'If we're going to live a full human life, we're going to feel the full range of human emotions. So let's stop calling them "positive" and "negative" emotions; instead let's call them "painful" or "pleasant".'

We are currently in the process of getting in touch with our values, setting goals, identifying changes to be made in your life. Learning and growing is an important part of life's journey, but it involves stepping out of your comfort zone and trying new things.

As soon as we step out of our comfort zone we feel discomfort. The most common form that takes is fear and anxiety. This goes right back to caveman days. Moving to unfamiliar territory was fraught with peril—new risks, less support, unknown dangers. Survival depended on strength and vigilance, and the fight or flight response—hard wiring that puts the body on standby to either fight or flee—kicks in. In the twenty-first century this manifests as fear or anxiety, and can be triggered by a broad range of things from job insecurity and rising interest rates to meeting new people or concern that the world is a scary place full of aggression and violence. In this kind of fight or flight mode your heart rate is quickening, your breath is coming faster and more shallow, your nervous system is increasing blood flow to the large muscles of your arms and legs so you are ready to run or fight and is shutting down the blood flow to your digestive and sexual organs.

We are easily weighed down by these fears, anxieties and similar painful emotions. Often they hold us back. We struggle with them, trying to suppress them or seeking distractions. Unfortunately this struggle with fear and anxiety only exacerbates it. All too often the things we do to try to make it go away, such as taking drugs, alcohol, cigarettes or junk food, or avoiding challenges, procrastinating on important decisions, or trying to distract ourselves through watching TV or surfing the net—and the list goes on and on—these have a negative influence on our health and well-being. We feel drained— exhausted by the very things we thought would help us.

Mindfulness provides a great set of tools to help us handle our emotions more effectively. Without becoming overwhelmed by them. Without fighting with them. Without struggling with them. Without letting them hold us back.

Dr Russ's mindfulness skill set

In *Making Australia Happy*, Dr Russ guided our volunteers through a series of exercises, derived from ACT, that develop three fundamental mindfulness skills:

1 *Connection*: connecting with your here and now experience, engaging fully through all five senses, (even if it seems mundane, boring, or unpleasant).
2 *Defusion*: seeing thoughts for what they are—nothing more or less than sounds, words, stories, pictures, bits of language passing through our heads—and letting them come and go without getting caught up with them.
3 *Expansion*: opening up and making room for your emotions, allowing them to freely flow through you without a struggle, whether they are pleasant or painful.

(Note: there are many different terms for these three mindfulness skills. These particular terms come from Dr Russ's book, *The Happiness Trap*.)

Connection

Paying attention to what is happening right here, right now is something we all do from time to time but not nearly often enough. We all have moments of mindfulness when we go on holiday and take in the beautiful scenery, or if we're in a foreign country and we start noticing all the different sights and sounds. Or someone prepares a fantastic meal and we savour the first few mouthfuls, really noticing the taste, the smell and the texture. But mostly we go around on automatic pilot, caught up on the treadmill of daily life. More often than not, we're watching television or chatting over meals, instead of paying attention to the food. When our kids are talking to us we are making shopping lists in our head.

Would you notice—and stop and listen to—a busker in the street? Or would you rush past, focused on a deadline or an upcoming meeting? When we arranged for one of the world's finest flautists to busk near Happiness HQ in Marrickville, most of our volunteers walked by without noticing. Not one stopped to listen, and only one gave her some money.

Mindfulness helps us to engage with what we are doing in the present moment, to appreciate things that we take for granted and even to find fulfilment and satisfaction in things that we usually deem dull and boring, like washing the dishes or ironing shirts. A simple mindfulness exercise illustrates the point.

Savouring: the sultana exercise

To learn to fully appreciate what you often take for granted, to notice the smallest details that you might have passed by, you are going to take five minutes to eat just one sultana. Be curious and open to the experience. You will be surprised at the variety of experience such a simple activity can support.

For many of the participants in *Making Australia Happy* this exercise was initially a real challenge. Cade hates sultanas and couldn't imagine spending five minutes relishing the experience. Ben predicted that his mind would wander, even before the experiment had begun!

Clicking the stop watch, Dr Russ asked participants to look at the sultana, to study it as if they'd had never seen one before. Try it.

Take a sultana. Give it a slight squeeze. Notice the texture. Hold it to your nose. Smell the sultana. Now bring it up to your ear and gently roll it in between your fingers and notice the sound it makes. Slow down and notice what happens as you put it on your lips. Feel the texture. Touch it with your tongue. Then slowly explore it as you put it in your mouth. Once inside your mouth, be aware of the taste, the texture and the sensations in your mouth as you roll it around, then chew and finally swallow. Focus on the sultana all the time, and as you do you will notice that lots of different thoughts keep popping up. Just let them come and go and keep focusing on the sultana. Close your eyes to heighten the experience. Notice the sound as you eat it. Savour the taste.

Natalia was surprised at how quickly the time went. 'It was interesting that it went so quickly. It only seemed like two or three minutes. I've still got it in my mouth now.' This is one of the key things with mindfulness. When we're very engaged and absorbed in what we're doing, time passes quickly. It just goes by when we're really in the moment. Natalia: 'I found when my eyes were closed that I was much more distracted by sounds.'

There are times when we really want to pay attention to sounds like when a flautist is playing or when our children are telling us something important, but at other times we can just let them fade into the background.

Ben: 'I held the sultana to my ear and it sounded like the static at the beginning of a LP record. That was striking!' You haven't failed the exercise if you can't 'hear' your sultana. Most sultanas make a tiny crackling noise when you squeeze them, but some don't.

Tony: 'My mind wandered off a couple of times. I just thought of a grapevine when I started chewing on it and that reminded me of a holiday I had with my wife in the Hunter Valley.'

Liz: 'I was interested in how the skin on the outside was quite tough and the inside was soft, and then the tongue hit the gritty bit in the centre, which I didn't like, and then I started sort of mapping my tastebuds in my mind. I found myself thinking about what clever little things they are; they even make wine! Then realised I was having a dialogue with myself about whether or not I was focusing on the sultana. That fascinated me being in there with the dialogue, and then I went back to focusing on the sultana.'

The mind is constantly claiming our attention as it runs through the memory bank making connections that lead from one story to another.

Most people drift off ten, twenty, thirty or more times doing this exercise, so don't be concerned when you do. You will constantly get caught up in thoughts about the sultana as opposed to the actual taste and texture. When you do, just pull yourself back to focusing on the sultana. This is the natural state of the human mind, pulling us out of our experience again and again and again. Mindfulness doesn't come naturally. We have to train our attention. We have to consciously develop mindfulness skills.

Everyday mindfulness homework

To really get to grips with this you'll need to put it into practice frequently over the next few weeks.

Choose three things that you do everyday as a matter of course and choose to do them mindfully. It doesn't matter what you choose. You can notice how it feels say in the shower with the water running over your back. Or when you are cooking—be aware of the smells, sounds and textures. Be fully engaged in the present.

You might choose the first thing from your regular daily routine—something that you normally tend to rush through on automatic pilot, like brushing your teeth or washing your face. Do it mindfully, be absolutely engaged and present in what you're doing. Be open and curious. Notice the sensations. When you drift off into your thoughts, bring yourself back to what is happening the moment you realise it.

Now pick one of your everyday little pleasant activities and do that mindfully. It might be your morning cup of coffee, eating a piece of chocolate, or the first mouthful of dinner. It might be hugging somebody you love. It might be listening to some beautiful music. It might actually be stopping to smell the roses. Whatever you choose, savour the experience and do it mindfully.

Finally, pick a chore that you have to do to make your day work. It might be a different chore each day or it might be the same chore every day. Something like ironing shirts or stacking the dishwasher or making the children's lunch or making your bed. Something that you usually think of as a bore and tend to rush through, or even try to distract yourself from by watching television or listening to radio. Do that mindfully. Really notice every little bit of body movement and every sight, sound, smell, the taste if relevant, that goes into that activity.

Make a note in your journal or diary of what you noticed and experienced and any thoughts or feelings that showed up.

Defusion

Another element of mindfulness is defusion—separating or detaching from your thoughts.

The inner critic is constantly churning out negative self-judgements. We can't stop them popping up, but we can learn to see them for what they are—meaningless words. The most common one of all is 'I'm not good enough.' That old chestnut! It comes in many guises. I'm fat, I'm old, I'm ugly, I'm stupid, I'm incompetent, I'm selfish, I'm lazy, I'm a workaholic, I'm boring, I'm unlikeable, I'm inadequate, I'm not as smart, as rich, as beautiful as other people.

You might think you are the only person in the world who thinks that way, but one of the best-kept secrets on the planet is that everyone has their own version of the 'I'm not good enough story'. Multiple versions, in fact. Whatever is most personal is also most common!

To illustrate how we can learn how to live with those thoughts and take the power out of them, try the following exercises, which Dr Russ worked through with the *Making Australia Happy* volunteers during the filming of the series.

Defusion exercises

Bring to mind a really nasty, negative self-judgement that the inner critic keeps labelling you with. Think of the last time you were

Labelling your emotions

A team from the University of California, Los Angeles (UCLA) explored the neurobiological evidence behind another one of the key mindfulness skills that we use in our eight-step program: dampening heightened emotions by giving them a name or a label.

They took a group of college students and presented them with a series of faces showing emotional expressions. They were required to match a label to each face from a choice of two words offered underneath each picture. Sometimes the words would describe an emotion, like angry or fearful. Sometimes it would be a name like Harry or Susan, indicating that the label was a matter of choosing the correct gender rather than the emotion.[*]

They found that the angry and fearful faces triggered brain activity in the amygdala, the area in the brain linked with perceiving emotions, but when the students put a name to the emotion, the amygdala was less active and another area in the brain—the prefrontal cortex—was more active.

Commenting on their study, Matthew Lieberman, associate professor of psychology at UCLA, said, 'When you put your feelings into words you're activating this prefrontal region and seeing a reduced response in the amygdala. It's like hitting the brakes when you see a yellow light when you are driving. When you put feelings into words you seem to be hitting the brakes on your emotional responses.'

According to the lead author of the UCLA study, research scientist David Cresswell, the team was able to establish that the participants with the most activity in the pre frontal cortex and the least activity in the amygdala were those who were more mindful. 'Our findings suggest that people who are more mindful bring all sorts of prefrontal resources to turn down the amygdala, and show an underlying neurological reason for how mindfulness meditation programs improve mood and health.'

[*] Creswell, J.D., Way, B.M., Eisenberger, N.I. et al., 'Neural correlates of dispositional mindfulness during affect labeling', *Psychosomatic Medicine*, vol. 69, 2007, pp. 560–5.

beating yourself up for something. What did your mind say about you or your body?

The volunteers came up with common labels. For Liz it was 'Inadequate'. Ben wrote 'Unworthy'. Cade chose 'Boring' and Rebekah said 'Selfish'. Stephen's was 'Slow', Tony's 'Lazy' and Natalia chose 'Disgusting' and Liz K, 'inadequate'.

Put that negative self-judgement into a short sentence, in the form 'I am X' or 'I'm not Y enough'—for example, 'I am fat' or 'I'm not smart enough'.

Next you'll need to really believe that thought for about twenty seconds. Buy into it. Believe it as much as you possibly can. This is so that you can then go on to learn how to step back and separate from it and see it for what it is: nothing more or less than words and pictures.

We're not interested in whether the thought is true or false. The purpose of learning to step back and see our thoughts for what they are is to assess whether they are helpful or useful. It might be more accurate to call these thoughts helpful or unhelpful, or useful or not useful, rather than negative or positive.

Ask yourself: do these thoughts help me be the person I want to be, live the life I want to live, do the things I want to do?

So now, for twenty seconds, close your eyes and believe this negative self-judgement (e.g. 'I'm stupid', 'I'm not good enough') as much as you possibly can. Notice what it feels like emotionally when you become embroiled and entangled in it. Next, repeat this thought to yourself, word for word the same, except now with this phrase in front of it: 'I'm having the thought that …' (for example, 'I'm having the thought that I'm unworthy'). Now repeat it again, with a slightly longer phrase: 'I notice I'm having the thought that …' (for example, 'I notice I'm having the thought that I'm incompetent').

What happened? Most people find they start to separate or distance from the thought, and it loses much of its impact.

Next, try these more playful defusion techniques. (For each technique, you can either use the same self-judgement as before or choose a different one.) First, bring the thought to mind, and for twenty seconds, buy into it and believe it as much as you can. Now, silently sing this thought to the tune of 'Happy Birthday'. Then, silently say this thought to yourself, but this time, hear it in the voice of a movie star, cartoon character or sports commentator. Try it in a couple of different voices, and see what happens.

Dr Russ took the volunteers through a couple of other playful defusion exercises. In one exercise they inhaled a mouthful of gas from a helium-filled balloon, then said their negative self-judgement out aloud. With their lungs full of helium, their voices sounded like squeaky chipmunks, and they were unable to take the self-judgement seriously. (In fact, most of them cracked up laughing.)

In another exercise, he asked them to write their negative self-judgement on a cardboard name tag and pin it on their chest. Then he asked them to imagine that they were at a cocktail party, meeting all the others for the first time. He asked them to go around and introduce themselves, using the label as if it were their name.

Cade and Ben introduced themselves with the following:

Cade (extending his hand): 'Hi, I'm boring.'

Ben (shaking his hand): 'Oh, hello, boring, I'm unworthy. Pleased to meet you.'

Here's how some of our volunteers responded to some of these exercises:

Ben: 'I felt the negative mantra all through my body, my mind, my chest my whole being. It's not pleasant. Unworthy for me goes hand in hand with inadequacy. I don't feel I can justify my own existence sometimes. It is all-consuming and often very hard to snap out of it. But listening to Bugs Bunny and Arnie Schwarzenegger talking about being unworthy diluted the power of it. I can even laugh about it now.'

Liz: 'I'm always feeling inadequate and guilty. I'm always going, "I'm not being a good enough friend because I'm not making the time to contact people, I shouldn't have yelled at the kids, I should have not rushed them out the door so fast", and always I should've, should've, should've. It's like a ball and chain. I want to get to a place where I feel satisfied and see that I can do things to the best of my ability, and it's good enough.

'I learnt today that these are just words. When I write them down I see them as words, and not as a part of me. I'm going to keep doing this and I think it will really assist me.'

This is what we're aiming to do with mindfulness. We're not trying to get rid of these thoughts. We're trying to be able to see them for what they are and let them come and go without allowing them to rule our lives. By the end of the series Natalia had learned to really value this defusion technique.

'My word was "disgusting". I keep the badge with that label in a drawer which I open a lot. It's funny because it's just become this word on a piece of paper, and I have a little bit of a giggle when I see it; it's lost its nasty powerful effect. I feel detached from it. It doesn't have that painful effect … I'm not using that word with myself any more; it's just a word.'

By the end of the exercise, the volunteers were no longer taking these self-judgements seriously. The thoughts had lost all their impact.

During the first half of the program finding happiness seemed unachievable for Liz. She was newly separated and bringing up two children on her own. As someone who was quite an anxious person, adjusting to this new role and keeping house and home together was plaguing her with anxiety.

Dr Russ worked through several mindfulness techniques with Liz to help her stop trying to control her anxieties and just let them be. One of those techniques is a classic meditation exercise that has been practised for thousands of years: meditation on the breath. Dr Russ took Liz to a beach to lead her through this meditation, but you can do it anywhere, any time, as long as you can make yourself comfortable and it is reasonably quiet.

The traditional pose is to sit cross-legged, but you don't have to as long as your back is upright. You can either fix on a spot or close your eyes, whichever you prefer.

For the next few breaths, focus on emptying your lungs, pushing all the air out of your lungs, and just allowing them to fill by themselves. Notice how once the lungs are empty, they automatically refill. There's no need to take a deep breath in. See if you can just let your lungs find their own natural rhythm. There's no need to control it. Just allow your breath to come and go. Notice it flowing in and out of your body, in much the same way as the waves flow on to the shore and back into the ocean.

Your aim for the next few minutes is to focus on your breath, to observe your breath as if you are a curious scientist who has never encountered breathing before. The idea is to notice every little nuance. Notice the air coming in and out of your nostrils. Notice the rise and fall of your ribcage. Notice the rise and fall of your abdomen. As you're doing this, your mind will try to distract you. Your mind is a master storyteller, and it will tell you all sorts of narratives to try to hook you and pull you out of the exercise.

You can't stop your mind from doing that. This is normal and natural, and it will keep happening. The moment you realise you've been hooked by a story or a distraction, simply acknowledge it, unhook yourself and come back to the breath.

The aim is to let your mind chatter away like it's a radio playing in the background. And just keep your attention on the breath. Let your thoughts come and go as if they're just cars driving past, and keep your attention on the breath, noticing it as it flows in and out.

As this exercise continues, the feelings and sensations in your body will change. Pleasant feelings and sensations might arise. Equally they might be uncomfortable or confronting ones.

The aim is to allow the feelings and sensations in your body to be exactly as they are. Don't try to control them or change them. Don't try to hold on to them or push them away. Just allow those feelings and sensations to be exactly as they are, and keep your attention on the breath.

If you encounter a difficult feeling, try to acknowledge it silently. Say to yourself, 'I am having a feeling of backache' or 'I am having a feeling of anxiety'; something that just acknowledges the feeling. Allow it to be there, and keep your attention on the breath.

Again and again and again, your mind will hook you and pull you out of the exercise. Remember, this is quite normal. In fact you're doing well if you last ten seconds before your mind hooks you and distracts you. The moment you realise it, acknowledge it's happened, unhook yourself and come back to the breath.

Expand your awareness further. Once you've followed your breath all the way in and all the way out, noticing the rise and fall of your abdomen and chest, simultaneously notice your body around the breath. Straighten your back, and get a sense of your arms and your legs, your head, neck and shoulders. Be aware of your body and your breathing at the same time.

Now expand your awareness even further. Be aware of your body and your breathing as well as all the sounds you can hear. Stay like this for while. When you are ready, open your eyes.

If you decide to make meditation a regular habit, start off gently and build up. Five minutes once or twice a day is a good start. You can build up from there. Ten minutes twice a day is a good and achievable goal for most people. There are no hard and fast rules on where and how to sit except that it is best not to do it lying down as you might well fall asleep!

Liz's reflections on mindful breathing: 'My mind hooked me a couple of times. I noticed various things, like my hair blowing in the breeze, then at one stage I wondered how close the water was getting, but these thoughts were fleeting. The one sensation which I had three times, I think, was heat. It was like an internal heat that started from my shoulders and went down my arms, and for a second I wondered if the sun had come out. But it was a different sensation from the sun heating up. It was internal. And when I had that thought, I brought my attention back to the breathing again. It was really helpful to concentrate on something, like the ribs moving up and down. I find that sometimes just concentrating on breathing's not enough.'

Liz's first effort was twelve minutes—far longer than she imagined. After she finished she opened her eyes and stretched, taking in the elements around her. She felt it would be reasonable to begin with five minutes at home everyday.

In this exercise, we concentrated on the breath, but we could have been concentrating on eating the sultana or brushing our teeth or ironing a shirt. You can apply mindfulness any time, anywhere.

Here's another mindfulness exercise, again from the ACT model, for defusing from thoughts.

Leaves on a stream exercise

Find a comfortable position. Close your eyes.

Imagine a stream, with leaves floating down (or a moving black strip). As thoughts appear, place them on the leaves and let them float past (or place them on the moving black strip and let it carry them past).

From time to time, your mind will hook you with an interesting thought, and pull you out of the exercise. That's normal. The moment you realise it has happened, gently acknowledge it, unhook yourself, and start the exercise again.

Do this once or twice a day for three to five minutes.

Expansion

Dr Russ describes expansion as a way to open up and make room for our emotions, to let them be as they are; to let them come, let them stay and let them go in their own good time. Struggling with painful emotions only intensifies them. Expansion is about allowing them to be present without investing any effort or energy in fighting them. This doesn't mean that you like, want or approve of a painful emotion; it simply means that you allow it to be present without a struggle. Paradoxically, as you do this, the emotion has much less influence on you.

There are three steps to expansion: observe—breathe—allow.

1 *Observe*: you observe the feeling in much the same way as you observed the sultana: notice where it is in your body; the shape, size, depth, temperature and so on.
2 *Breathe*: you 'breathe into' the feeling. It's as if your breath flows into and around the feeling.
3 *Allow*: you allow the feeling to be there. You don't have to like it or want it; you just allow it.

This next exercise will be difficult, because we are suggesting that you deliberately evoke some difficult or painful memory in order to generate a painful emotion. But if you are willing to do that, you will be able to practise the expansion exercise and learn a valuable skill that will help you deal with similar feelings in the future.

Sit in a upright position with your feet pressed firmly on the floor. Either close your eyes or fix on a spot, whichever you prefer. Take a moment to notice how you're sitting. Notice your body posture. Notice the different sounds that you can hear coming from inside the room and from outside the room. Notice what your mind is telling you.

For the next few breaths just focus on emptying your lungs, pushing all the air out of your lungs, and allowing them to fill by themselves.

Bring to mind a memory that is associated with some sort of painful emotion for you—fear, anger, sadness, guilt, anxiety.

What can you see? What can you hear? What are you doing with your arms and your legs? Go right back into that situation and see whether you can get in touch with whatever it brings up for you. Get in touch with that anger or that sadness or that fear or that anxiety or hurt.

Dr Russ worked through this exercise with Liz. For her it was the anxiety she always feels when she is trying to get the kids off to school and they are dragging their feet.

'It happens to me all the time,' said Liz. 'My daughter takes forty minutes to eat one piece of toast, and I get really angry.'

'Make room for that feeling,' said Dr Russ. 'Let it be there without struggling with it. Just breathe into it. Let your breath flow into and around the feeling. If you like, place a hand on it. See if you can hold it gently. This is just a bit of the past showing up in the present. You've got a long history of being pushed around by this feeling, but you don't have to fight with it or struggle with it. Just breathe into it, open up around it, just let it be there. You don't have to like it or want it. Just see if you can allow it to be there so that, instead of struggling with it, you can put your energy into being with your kids.'

Liz practised this exercise many times. She found that she automatically visualised her feeling like a tight coil inside her. She imagined that the coil opened up, allowing her breath to flow through it, so she could stop struggling with the feeling and live with it.

At the same time she was learning to detach from her inner critic chastising her for running late. 'It doesn't have so much clout any more,' said Liz. 'It is not the big, booming roar that it used to be. I can actually accept that it's not changing anyone's life if I turn up fifteen or twenty minutes late for something. Probably I am the only one who notices.'

Dr Russ continued: 'There'll be times when your mind hooks you and pulls you back into old self-defeating habits. And there'll be times when you realise it and you unhook yourself and you breathe and you become mindful and you come back to your values. It will be an ongoing process. You're never going to be perfect, but what you can do is get better and better at realising you've been hooked by that dictatorial inner voice so you can unhook yourself, get present, come back, be mindful.'

Just like Liz, learn to scan your body.

Body scan

Start at the top of your head and work downwards. Notice the different sensations that you can feel in your forehead, your eyes and so on.

Zoom in on the part of your body where you feel this emotion most intensely. Observe that part of your body as if you are a curious scientist who has never encountered a sensation or feeling like this before.

Breathe into and around the feeling. As you do this, imagine that in some magical way you expand. All this space opens up inside you, around the feeling, giving it plenty of room to move.

The feeling might increase, decrease or disappear. There is no way to predict what it will do. While the feeling is still present, notice that you are in full control of your actions. Move your arms and your legs to check this out for yourself. As long as you are mindful, you can have the most intense emotions, but you can take control of your arms and your legs and your mouth, and act and behave the way you want to, regardless of the feelings that are present.

The object of the exercise is to learn to live with our feelings and to get on with what we want to do in our lives—acting on our values and pursuing our goals, even when difficult feelings arise in the process.

Until recently, we had to do long meditation courses to learn how to detach ourselves from unhelpful thoughts and drop the struggle with painful feelings. But exercises like these teach us how to do this very quickly. And they work.

Mindfulness skills can be quickly and easily learned without the need for formal meditation, and our volunteers demonstrated this very dramatically. Not only did their levels of happiness increase but also the brain scans that they had taken before and after the eight-week program showed interesting changes. There is more on this in Part 3, 'The Science'.

Step 4: Strengths and solutions

Imagine that three people—a botanist, a geologist and an architect—go for a walk together in a national park. What does each see? What do they talk about?

The botanist is enthralled. He sees an abundance of wildlife everywhere. His attention is captured. He finds himself appreciating the diversity of the plant life. With relish he notes the number of different plant and insect species. He starts to think about conservation. On the other hand, the geologist finds herself captivated by the number of different rocks and soils evident in the park. To her, each distant rocky outcrop, each rock formation tells a different story and each gives her subtle but powerful clues as to how the landscape was formed over the years. She finds her attention being drawn to the texture of the soil underfoot, the number of different types of stones lying by the pathway on which they walk. She finds herself wondering about how the rainwater would have shaped the gullies on the side of the hill and speculating as to whether there might be mineral deposits in the distant mountain range. In contrast, the architect's mind automatically turns to thoughts of how a beautiful suburb could be built there. In her mind's eye she sees houses with magnificent views and safe quiet streets for children to ride their bikes in.

She sees families and friends socialising. She envisages ecologically friendly, community-based living. She feels inspired by the rise and fall of the dramatic vista and automatically starts to think about how she could incorporate elements into a current design project. She decides to start drafting some ideas as soon as she returns to the office. As they walk along, the group falls silent. Each of the three is lost in their own thoughts, lost in their own private experience of the national park.

Our mindsets—our frames of reference—have a major influence on what we notice and how we experience the world. Each of these three had a very different mindset, and each had a very different experience of the national park.

Our mindsets can determine how successful we are in life. People with a 'fixed' mindset that says that success is dependent on innate ability are less likely to continue working hard in the face of setbacks than those with a 'growth' mindset—which says that success is based on hard work and effort. Not surprisingly, a 'growth' mindset is associated with greater achievement.[1]

Incredible as it might seem, a mindset can even bring about physical changes. A remarkable study showed that people who think exercise is doing them good will actually benefit more, physically, than people without any expectations. The job of being a hotel chambermaid involves a lot of physical exertion. A group of hotel chambermaids who were informed that the work that they did was both good exercise and satisfied the recommended requirements for an active lifestyle showed a decrease in weight, blood pressure, body fat, waist-to-hip ratio, and body mass index after four weeks. The comparison group who did the same amount of physical activity did not experience those benefits.[2]

Although mindsets are fundamentally critical in shaping our experience of the world, we rarely pay attention to them. We rarely stop and think about our frames of reference. We rarely think about whether we tend to focus on the positive, the negative or nothing in particular. We rarely think about our thinking at all.

Step 4 is about cultivating a mindset that will help us achieve the goals to which we aspire and to overcome the seemingly insurmountable obstacles along the way, vital to fulfilling our happiness potential. We do it by learning to look for solutions to problems rather than becoming bogged down in the problems themselves while drawing on a pot-pourri of strengths, talents and abilities that we might not even have realised we had.

The strengths-based and solution-focused approach

The notion of strengths and solutions is central to Positive Psychology. Much of clinical and counselling psychology in the past has focused on how to help people with mental illness or life problems overcome those difficulties and lead normal productive lives. This has been an important aspect of psychology. Psychology has revealed how depression and anxiety develop, how depression persists with certain thinking styles and how to help people recover. There has been much less focus within clinical and counselling psychology about the positive aspects of people. Until recently one could go through an undergraduate degree in psychology and then complete postgraduate training—more than six years of full-time study—and still not learn about how to bring out the best in people.

Strengths-based and solution-focused approaches focus on what is good about the individual, what works. These approaches seek to create purposeful positive change by amplifying the strengths or good points of the person, rather than finding the weakness or dysfunctions and fixing those. In this way it is quite a radical departure from the medical model of problem diagnosis and treatment.

The simple idea underpinning this is that 'what you focus on grows'. If we focus on fear, threat or danger, that is what our minds tend to become attuned to spotting. It's like listening to a dripping tap at night. As we find ourselves focusing on it, the sound seems to get louder and louder. In much the same way, if we train ourselves to focus on strengths, we can reorient our minds to the positive.

It is important to emphasise that we are not advocating unrealistic 'happy-dappy' positive thinking—this is not about looking only at the positive. It is not about saying that people are 'not allowed' to have disturbing, unhappy or depressing thoughts. Many life situations naturally provoke distress and anxiety. We need to be able to experience a full range of emotions, both positive and negative. An unrealistic and inauthentic approach to a strengths-based and solution-focused approach can have the effect of making unhappy people feel guilty or depressed about having so-called negative thoughts. The kind of dictatorial approach that says people should only have happy thoughts, or should only treat painful life events as 'blessings', is not what we are advocating. Often we need to be able to accept and learn to embrace negative events in our lives in order to make real change in our lives.

What we are saying is that being able to focus purposefully on strengths and solutions brings with it flexibility in thinking and mindset. Flexibility in being able to make choices. Flexibility in how we experience the world. And, to our way of thinking, flexibility entails freedom.

Understanding character strengths

Character strengths are a very useful framework for understanding ourselves. In many ways they epitomise the core of Positive Psychology. Those aspects of ourselves at our best. Our strengths.

To create their seminal work *Character Strengths and Virtues*,[3] Martin Seligman and Christopher Peterson mined the major religious and philosophical traditions of the world looking for a definitive and ubiquitous set of strengths and virtues that human beings need to thrive. They came up with six overarching virtues that almost every culture in the world endorses—wisdom and knowledge, courage, humanity, justice, temperance and transcendence—and, under these broad categories, twenty-four distinct strengths ranging from creativity and wisdom to honesty and perseverance, social intelligence, fairness, modesty and humility, humour and spirituality and hope (see the boxed text).

Character strengths

Wisdom and knowledge: cognitive strengths that entail the acquisition and use of knowledge

- Creativity [originality, ingenuity]: thinking of novel and productive ways to conceptualise and do things; includes artistic achievement but is not limited to it

- Curiosity [interest, novelty-seeking, openness to experience]: taking an interest in ongoing experience for its own sake; finding subjects and topics fascinating; exploring and discovering

- Judgement and open-mindedness [critical thinking]: thinking things through and examining them from all sides; not jumping to conclusions; being able to change one's mind in light of evidence; weighing all evidence fairly

- Love of learning: mastering new skills, topics, and bodies of knowledge, whether on one's own or formally; obviously related to the strength of curiosity but goes beyond it to describe the tendency to add systematically to what one knows

- Perspective [wisdom]: being able to provide wise counsel to others; having ways of looking at the world that make sense to oneself and to other people

Courage: emotional strengths that involve the exercise of will to accomplish goals in the face of opposition, external or internal

>

- Bravery [valour]: not shrinking from threat, challenge, difficulty or pain; speaking up for what is right even if there is opposition; acting on convictions even if unpopular; includes physical bravery but is not limited to it
- Perseverance [persistence, industriousness]: finishing what one starts; persisting in a course of action in spite of obstacles; 'getting it out the door'; taking pleasure in completing tasks
- Honesty [authenticity, integrity]: speaking the truth but more broadly presenting oneself in a genuine way and acting in a sincere way; being without pretence; taking responsibility for one's feelings and actions
- Zest [vitality, enthusiasm, vigour, energy]: approaching life with excitement and energy; not doing things halfway or half-heartedly; living life as an adventure; feeling alive and activated

Humanity: interpersonal strengths that involve tending and befriending others

- Capacity to love and be loved: valuing close relations with others, in particular those in which sharing and caring are reciprocated; being close to people
- Kindness [generosity, nurturance, care, compassion, altruistic love, 'niceness']: doing favours and good deeds for others; helping them; taking care of them
- Social intelligence [emotional intelligence, personal intelligence]: being aware of the motives and feelings of other people and oneself; knowing what to do to fit into different social situations; knowing what makes other people tick

Justice: civic strengths that underlie healthy community life

- Teamwork [citizenship, social responsibility, loyalty]: working well as a member of a group or team; being loyal to the group; doing one's share
- Fairness: treating all people the same according to notions of fairness and justice; not letting personal feelings bias decisions about others; giving everyone a fair chance

>

- Leadership: encouraging a group of which one is a member to get things done and at the same time maintain good relations within the group; organising group activities and seeing that they happen

Temperance: strengths that protect against excess

- Forgiveness and mercy: forgiving those who have done wrong; accepting the shortcomings of others; giving people a second chance; not being vengeful
- Modesty and humility: letting one's accomplishments speak for themselves; not regarding oneself as more special than one is
- Prudence: being careful about one's choices; not taking undue risks; not saying or doing things that might later be regretted
- Self-regulation [self-control]: regulating what one feels and does; being disciplined; controlling one's appetites and emotions

Transcendence: strengths that forge connections to the larger universe and provide meaning

- Appreciation of beauty and excellence [awe, wonder, elevation]: noticing and appreciating beauty, excellence, and/or skilled performance in various domains of life, from nature to art to mathematics to science to everyday experience
- Gratitude: being aware of and thankful for the good things that happen; taking time to express thanks
- Hope [optimism, future-mindedness, future orientation]: expecting the best in the future and working to achieve it; believing that a good future is something that can be brought about
- Humour [playfulness]: liking to laugh and tease; bringing smiles to other people; seeing the light side; making (not necessarily telling) jokes
- Religiousness and spirituality [faith, purpose]: having coherent beliefs about the higher purpose and meaning of

>

the universe; knowing where one fits within the larger scheme; having beliefs about the meaning of life that shape conduct and provide comfort.

All of us have a number of these strengths to a greater or lesser degree, but it's the ones at which you excel, the ones that provide you with a sense of invigoration and comfort within yourself, that are of most value.

Character strengths have three important components: (1) they are core aspects of our character; (2) they are patterns of thoughts, feelings and behaviour that come naturally to us and feel authentic, and (3) we feel energised and alive when we are using our own strengths.[4]

The idea is to identify our top five strengths and to start to use them in our daily lives. A number of websites provide a vehicle to identify your strengths. Go to www.viacharacter.org or follow the link from the *Making Australia Happy* website at www.abc.net.au/makingaustraliahappy. To complete these online you will need to fill out a survey that provides the framework for your personalised top-five signature strengths profile. It takes about thirty to forty minutes to complete.

Identifying our own set of personal strengths and working with them to bring about change in our lives is a very powerful tool and an important part of the strengths-based approach. It's like changing a lens in your camera. Changing focus lets us take on a new perspective and give up, at least temporarily, our old ways of thinking.

Once you have defined your top five strengths, you can practise using one of them in a new and different way every day for a week. For example, if 'love of learning' is one of your top strengths, start collecting articles in your area of interest and build up a file. If 'loving and allowing yourself to be loved' is one of your strengths, think of some innovative ways to express this. Something as simple as telephoning a friend or relative whom you've neglected recently might be profoundly effective.

Seligman and his colleagues have shown that identifying your five key character strengths and then using one of them in a new way each day for a week can reduce depression and increase happiness for up to six months.[5]

When Liz K discovered that her top strength was social intelligence it shifted the way she thought about certain things. Socially intelligent people are aware of their own motives and feelings and the motives and feelings of others. They know what makes other people tick, and they are good at fitting into different social situations. Liz K knew she was strong in these qualities, but she had allowed herself to get into the habit of trying to please everybody to her own self-detriment. Accepting that you have to be nice to yourself and take time out for yourself before you can be there for other people actually enhanced her relationships with her friends and family.

Natalia discovered that curiosity and appreciation of beauty were two of her top five strengths. Curious people are open to experience, on the lookout for new and interesting things. They love to explore and discover, taking an interest in experience for its own sake; finding subjects and topics fascinating. The scope for appreciating beauty is wide, taking in music, the arts, nature, mathematics, science. Indeed many people find beauty in small everyday experience.

Natalia had taken these character traits for granted in the past. She went out photographing her local neighbourhood, which made her realise that knowing her own character strengths and acting on them could really enhance her life.

Tony's top strength was gratitude. While he was aware of, and thankful for, the good things in his life, he was not taking the time to express his thanks. He was so caught up in the stresses and strains of the daily round of work and family commitments that he was neglecting this area entirely, especially at work. He decided to reward his staff by taking them out to dinner and booked a table at the local Greek taverna. Over dinner, he gave a brief speech thanking every staff member for their hard work and their participation in helping the office grow.

The staff were, of course, delighted. 'We all feel a little more appreciated after tonight. When your boss recognises the hard work that you've been doing and thanks you in front of the rest of the team it makes you want to strive even harder to get noticed, so it's good.'

Strangely, it can be quite threatening and downright disconcerting to try looking at the world purposefully and to understand oneself through a strengths focus. It means taking on a new perspective. Looking anew. Thinking anew. It means giving up (at least temporarily) one's old ways of thinking.

Not surprisingly, this can be scary. We may find that some of our dearly loved assumptions about the world are not true. Therein lies a paradox. People who are relatively happy may find it harder to switch to a strengths viewpoint than those who are relatively unhappy. If we are depressed or distressed it may be that we feel we have nothing to lose. In this sense the good may well be the enemy of the great! So, if you find it difficult to make the switch to a strengths-based mindset, don't worry. You are in good company.

In Tony's case the dinner was a catalyst that set him on a different course. He realised that seeing the world through the gratitude lens had a further spin-off. 'I used to be angry or cranky with the staff. I used to focus on the negative. Now I don't. When I do get upset I say to myself, "OK, they're good staff, they're positive, stay positive." And when I do speak to them, I speak to them in a nicer tone and I encourage them and I say, "Look, this is where you went wrong, don't worry, let's do it again, you're great at this, you're good at this." That came from Dr Tony. Just to practise on their strengths.'

From strengths to solution-focused

The strengths-based approach is specifically about applying one's character strengths to a situation. The solution-focused approach is about combining those strengths with what we know about the individual's circumstances, finding out what works for the individual and then doing more of that.

We look to the future, rather than the present or the past: what would we like to have happen? The focus is on how to fix a problem rather than on why we've got one.

In short, we advocate a strong combination of both. In fact we see a combined strengths–solution approach as being central to purposeful positive change. Several key assumptions underpin the solution-focused approach. These are:

- A focus on constructing solutions: the focus is primarily on the construction of solutions rather than trying to understand the aetiology of the problem. Ask yourself 'how to'—not 'why'.
- A focus on potential, not pathology: don't look at life difficulties and problems as being signs of pathology or dysfunctionality. Try to see them as stemming from a limited repertoire of behaviour—we just need to learn how to do things differently. You are the expert on your own life: You have a unique understanding of yourself. Experts' views are useful, but you know yourself best.
- Clear, specific goal setting: set clear and attainable goals, and set yourself a specific time frame.
- The assumption that change can happen in a short period of time: you don't need a long time to make change happen. Small steps can create change quickly.
- A future orientation: focus more on the future (what you want to have happen) rather than the present or the past.

A solution-focused mindset

One of the key aspects of this solution-focused approach is having an open mind, a positive expectation that change will happen. And it's true. Change happens all the time.

With a positive solutions-focused mindset we are looking to make small steps in a positive direction, small things that will make a positive difference. It may be possible to make really big changes, and if that is so—great! But it does not matter how small the change is, and it doesn't have to be exactly the change we plan. What matters is the positive mindset that sustainable change can and will occur.

There is very good reason to think that a solution-focused approach is useful in creating purposeful positive change. Randomised controlled research studies have shown that solution-focused coaching

The solution-focused mindset

The power of the solution-focused mindset demonstrated in the *Making Australia Happy* bowling scenario was based on a famous ten-pin bowling study at the University of Wisconsin.[*]

In this study Dr Daniel Kirschenbaum wanted to explore the effects of positive and negative mindsets. He took a large group of ten-pin bowlers and split them into different groups. Both group A and group B received instruction from a professional coach, including a description and a demonstration of the seven key components of effective bowling. They were all issued with self-monitoring forms to keep track of their performance. They were instructed to monitor their performance after each frame of play with reference to the seven core skills. Group A, the 'positive self-monitoring group', were instructed to mark themselves as good, very good or excellent against the skills they had done well and to ignore the rest. Group B, the 'negative self-monitoring group', were told to make a note of their errors on a scale of poor, very poor and terrible and to concentrate on avoiding making the same mistakes in the following rounds.

Incredibly, the bowlers who focused on what they did well improved their bowling averages as much as 100 per cent compared to the group that concentrated on their weaknesses.

[*] Kirschenbaum, D.S., Ordman, A.M., Tomarken, A.J. et al., 'Effects of differential self-monitoring and level of mastery on sports performance: Brain power bowling', *Cognitive Therapy and Research*, vol. 6, 1982, pp. 335–41.

can help a wide range of people, including executives[6] and high school students,[7] to enhance their well-being and performance. Moreover, compared to questions that explore the problem (problem-focused questions), a solution-focused approach has been shown to be more effective at increasing goal progression and enhancing positive affect.[8]

The *Making Australia Happy* series took the volunteers ten-pin bowling to demonstrate the power of the solution-focused positive mindset. None of them was a skilled bowler. The local coach demonstrated the four core skills that, once mastered, can turn a novice into a reasonable bowler in no time. We told both groups that the aim of the evening was to improve their skills and that we would be asking them to assess their own progress during the evening.

Then we split them randomly into two groups of four and separated them at opposite ends of the bowling alley. Both teams had to keep track of their performance. But each was told to track something different. We told group A, the blue team, to concentrate on what they were doing well and group B, the red team, to watch out for their mistakes and to avoid making the same mistakes in the subsequent rounds. After each bowl, team members in group A were to mark their success and rate themselves on a scale of good, very good and excellent. But team B were told to log their errors—from poor, very poor to terrible. Dr Tony increased the pressure by moving between the teams playing the supportive coach with team A and criticising team B's errors.

By the end of the evening Team A was ahead by a remarkable fifteen points!

Just as developing a positive mindset to build on our strengths can help with short-term goals like learning to bowl, it's also a powerful way to envisage and accomplish the longer-term goals to which we aspire.

How do we do solution-focused change?

The first thing is to decide to use solution-focused mindset. Ask yourself: am I ready to buy a solution, or am I still too attached to the problem?

These are some tested ways of creating solution-focused change:

Highlighting times when the problem does not exist

Highlighting times when the problem does not exist and using this as a clue to do more of what works in such a situation sounds obvious, but we frequently keep trying to solve problems by using the same (failed) solutions. Insanity, as they say, is doing the same thing but expecting different results!

Natalia recognised that she was neglecting herself physically and mentally, mainly because she was putting in long hours at work. She was passionate and committed to social work but recognised that ten-hour days or more without a break was not sustainable. 'The work itself is pretty full on and it's emotionally draining, but the worst thing about it is that I could work there twenty-four hours a day and still not be on top of it.'

The conventional therapeutic approach is to explore the reason why Natalia appears to be a workaholic. The solution-based approach looks at whether she has been able to keep her workload under control in the past, and see whether we can find some ways to recapture how she managed to do that.

Natalia recollected the time when she first began the job. 'I switched offices and really went in with this idea—quite focused—that I was going to make this a really healthy change. I joined a gym and was eating my lunch away from my desk. I was leaving at maybe five or five-thirty.'

Initially Natalia had found it easy to leave early because she was not yet familiar with the enormity of the caseload. She was able to focus on things that she had to do as opposed to the things that she could do. Dr Tony suggested that that is still the reality of her workload; she still has to focus on things that she has to do rather than things that she could do. Together in a coaching session they identified strategies that she could put into place so that she could re-create that era, such as drawing up a list first thing in the morning of the priorities for that day; setting an alarm to remind her to leave work early; creating diary entries for 'me time' to give herself some space so that she would return to her work refreshed and energised and, most importantly, to treat herself the way she would expect to be treated by a considerate employer. Her long hours were self-imposed.

By the end of the series, Natalia felt a little more in control and able to set up priorities a little better, although 'I'm still struggling with being a good boss to myself,' she said.

Keep it small and simple

Take small, easily achievable steps that build in time to overall stretching goals, rather than overwhelming yourself with large initial actions. This tactic worked for Ben.

He was desperate to develop meaningful relationships and introduce some creativity and adventure into his life. 'I want to change a whole bunch of stuff, and I wish I could make a decision about what to do and have the guts to take action.' But he had a $15 000 debt hanging over him, which was holding him back from taking any action at all. 'I became very hedonistic. I went out and did as much as I could and didn't care about the repercussions of anything I was doing.'

Dr Tony suggested small practical steps to help him reach those bigger goals:

1 Clean up the spare room in his flat.
2 Rent it out.
3 Get financial advice.

It took Ben a few weeks, but eventually he took the first steps. 'I'm not quite sure what flipped the switch inside me to attack it and engage in the activities. But I think you get to a point where you realise you can't wallow in your situation forever.'

He did clean up the room, he did advertise for a flatmate, and he did make an appointment to see a financial adviser.

'I want to go overseas and meet people and maybe work or volunteer in some way. And having that in mind is going to be a really good tool to help me get through the financial problems that I have and pay off that debt—because that's the whole point, isn't it? To create this freedom so that I can go and explore and meet people. The motivation is there. It's itching. So I'm committed.'

Solution-focused coaching in the workplace

Dr Tony Grant and his colleagues at Sydney University have other examples of how a solution focus can be a powerful driver of change. A 2009 study of solution-focused coaching in the workplace found that, compared to a control group, the executives who went through the solution-focused coaching program had more success achieving their goals, greater increases in resilience and workplace well-being and reduced depression and stress.[*] They also reported feeling more self-confident and insightful, and better able to improve their management skills and deal with organisational change.

The solution-focused approach also works in schools. In another randomised controlled study, a group of 16-year-olds at a girls high school in Sydney took part in an evidence-based life coaching program.[†] After ten individual coaching sessions the group who had had the benefit of coaching showed fewer depressive symptoms and greater hope and resilience.

Another study run by the UK Centre for Positive Psychology invited 240 students to select their top five strengths at the beginning of term, then to select three personal goals they would like to achieve during that term. They were specifically instructed to use their strengths to help them achieve those goals. The strategy worked. When students used their strengths in trying to achieve their goals, they made better progress than when not using those strengths.[‡]

[*] Grant, A.M., Curtayne, L. & Burton, G., 'Executive coaching enhances goal attainment, resilience and workplace well-being: A randomised controlled study', *Journal of Positive Psychology*, vol. 4, 2009, pp. 396–407.

[†] Green, L.S., Grant, A.M. & Rynsaardt, J., 'Evidence-based life coaching for senior high school students: Building hardiness and hope', *International Coaching Psychology Review*, vol. 2, 2007, pp. 24–32.

[‡] Linley, P.A., Nielsen, K.M., Gillett, R. et al., 'Using signature strengths in pursuit of goals: Effects on goal progress, need satisfaction, and well-being, and implications for coaching psychologists', *International Coaching Psychology Review*, vol. 5, 2010, pp. 6–15.

Rate your progress on a 1 to 10 scale

Scaling is a versatile way of subjectively measuring experience, and can be used in many different ways. We move towards our goal step by step, and each time we ask ourselves: what would it take to get to the next point on the scale? Remember, you only need to move up by one point at a time. Small steps add up big feats!

Look out for hidden resources

It is amazing how often a presenting problem holds unrecognised strengths and resources. It is a cliché, but true, that every problem is the seed of its solution.

One reason Ben was able to flip the switch was that he learned to draw on inner resources that he didn't know he had. He thought he was incapable of making decisions. But a coaching session with Dr Tony helped him take a different perspective. When Dr Tony took him through a typical day in the life of Ben he could see that he was actually quite used to making decisions. Even something apparently as mundane as choosing to go and hear Band A rather than Band B, then booking the ticket, involves a process of confident decision-making.

Cade was desperate to get out of his repetitive and monotonous job as a TV scheduler and into production, but was scared of making the move, most of all because he feared failure. Dr Tony showed him that instead of focusing on all the things he was afraid of, he could be proactive by drawing on his own enormous pool of creative resources. Cade's hobby and passion is making video clips that he publishes on the internet. Dr Tony encouraged Cade to think about his search for a new job as a great metaphor, in fact as a movie. They called it *Cade's Excellent Adventure: Trials and Tribulations of a Job Seeker*. He, 'Big Cade', would be the director of the movie about 'Little Cade'.

As they discussed the story of the film and developed the imaginary shooting script, Cade found that he was coming up with a real plan of action. He saw that he had the skills to make a promo reel that he could show to potential employers; he had contacts in the industry from whom he could solicit help and support; and he could even face being turned down because he has already experienced having some of his hobby pieces rejected online and it is not the end of the world.

Getting a job in production now seemed like an achievable goal. 'Seeing it as if it was a little movie, breaking it down into bite-sized chunks, as opposed to seeing it as a massive mountain, made it feel completely achievable,' said Cade. 'It's a bit of a light at the end of the tunnel that's just opened up so that's very exciting.'

Possibility language

Possibility language involves talking about your problems in a way that fosters discovery of potential solutions. A well-known technique is the 'Magic Question' in which you can ask yourself (something like): 'Imagine that I went to bed tonight, and when I woke up the problem had somehow magically disappeared, and the solution was present … but you didn't know that the solution had arrived … what is the first thing that I'd notice that would tell me that the solution was present?' If you find that language a bit clumsy or fanciful, a useful variation is the 'What if' question: if things were going a bit better, what would be different?

Stephen wanted more spare time and more time with his family. But he couldn't see how he could achieve that without his work suffering. It was making him very unhappy. However, when asked to imagine what his day might look like if things were different, he painted a scenario that turned out to be very doable.

'That ideal day would mean I'd get up and not be thinking how early can I get to work or what do I need to do at work. I'd be thinking do some exercise, give something to my body. I'd be more relaxed. My demeanour would be more open. It would give me more foundations for building things with the family and communicating at work.'

By the end of the eight weeks Stephen had committed himself to coming home early from work at least one day every week in time to have supper with the family. He had started walking three mornings a week before work, taking his son running and playing tennis and golf. He felt more relaxed, and his family and colleagues pronounced him chirpier and more communicative.

The 'letter from the future'

The ultimate tool for creating possibilities is to write yourself a letter from the future.

We asked Liz to do this exercise. We encouraged her to dream really big. She found it to be a very powerful experience which helped her see that the future was not nearly as scary a prospect as she was always imagining, particularly since splitting up with her partner.

In the letter she allowed herself to dream of meeting a new partner and of financial security, perhaps opening her own naturopathy practice, playing lots of competition sport but also continuing on a spiritual path with yoga and meditation. When she had finished writing the letter we had it written up as a magazine article, and gave it back to her as a reminder and a memento.

Reading it back, she realised that everything she had dreamed was achievable and all it required was to start to make small changes. One step at a time. 'I don't know what my future holds, but seeing all these ideas on the page—I realise that it is all feasible, all doable,' she said. 'I have started to consider taking on some study … just a few hours a week that I can fit in without too much pressure … it could be naturopathy. It will definitely be something spiritual. I don't know what my future holds, but I really do feel positive about it and I do believe that good things will come my way.'

Star of 2010 ABC TV series reveals her dream life

Once wracked with anxiety, naturopath Liz has finally found personal serenity.

At age 45, life is only getting better for Liz. The devoted mother of two teenagers has overcome many of the mental and financial challenges she's battled with for decades, and has finally come into her own.

A resident of Sydney's inner west, Liz owns her own home in a quiet Newtown cul-de-sac and lives with her 16-year-old son and 14-year-old daughter. Both children are model students, and her son was recently awarded a creative achievement for his work on a school building project—a talent that has been evident from an early age. Liz is thrilled by his success, and supportive of his drive to run a building company.

A successful naturopath with a thriving practice in the local area, she is renowned for her openness and non-judgemental attitude. She routinely treats all walks of the community with her specialised therapies and has even established a weekly restorative clinic for underprivileged kids from low socio-economic families.

Working in natural health is the perfect complement to Liz's passion for health and fitness. She has long subscribed to running and weight training, and is currently preparing for the Noosa triathlon. With several races under her belt already, she will no doubt be a tough competitor to beat in the over-forties category.

Life wasn't always so rosy for Liz, though. With the loss of her father at an early age, and her mother to cancer when she was only 22, her early life was tough. She also struggled for more than a decade with an eating disorder, which led to prolonged anxiety and control issues.

It was her appearance in the 2010 ABC TV series *Making Australia Happy* that gave her the impetus to make a serious commitment to transforming her life. At the time, she had just broken up from her marriage with a partner of twelve years, had financial troubles and was plagued by a persistent feeling there

>

was something missing in her life. She yearned for some kind of inner peace and tranquillity, which would equate to satisfaction and happiness.

Prompted to address her various issues, Liz took her life into her own hands and faced her demons head on. Having long sacrificed her own self-exploration and individual desires in order to give her all to personal relationships, she finally took the time to scrutinise herself in detail and—all clichés aside— find herself.

Realising she needed to connect her mind more with her body, she enrolled in yoga, quickly discovering its healing and revitalising potential. She went on to master the Iyengar form and explore the more athletic Ashtanga, not only reaping the physical benefits but also drawing on the spiritual dimensions in her quest for inner peace. Fortuitously it was through yoga classes that she met her current partner and soulmate, also a triathlete, with whom she now trains and competes. She credits yoga and meditation with helping her to have confidence in her own abilities and to stop worrying about the opinions of others.

Although she didn't have the opportunity to travel much until her late thirties due to her financial and family constraints, Liz was determined to broaden her horizons. Her eventual return to her native Poland was a cultural awakening that reconnected her with her roots. Her soul-searching led her through Rome, the Greek Islands and greater Europe, culminating with a trip to India, in the pursuit of higher yoga practice and spiritual knowledge.

These days, through her pursuit of naturopathy, yoga and painting, an expression of creativity she only recently discovered, Liz has attained the work–life balance, financial security and ability to relax that had eluded her for most of her life. It's been a long road on her quest for serenity but, having reached this point, she isn't looking back.

How to write your letter

Chose a date in the future. Make it at least three months time—it could be up to several years. Imagine that you had travelled forward in time to this date and you are now sitting down writing a letter to yourself describing how your life has changed, how you managed to get rid of the things that bugged you, how you became happier.

When you write this letter, rather than focusing on the negative—the things that drag you down—try focusing on your character strengths. Focus on your personal strengths and write about how they have helped you make positive change. Make sure you include your core values. You might like to go back to Step 1: Goals and values and see what you thought about there.

In the letter describe what is happening in your life. What you are thinking and feeling. What you are doing. What you are enjoying. Write about every life domain you can think of. Health, finances, romance, career, travel—the lot! Write about whatever is most relevant for you. Write about how your needs and values are being met and how these are motivating you.

You might also like to write about how you created these changes. Be as detailed as you can. Allow your mind to roam.

The 'letter from the future' is a simple and powerful tool for change. Over the years it has been used with many thousands of people.[9] And it works not only with people who see themselves as being 'creative' types but also by an incredibly wide range of personality types, including elite Royal Australian Air Force test pilots, captains of industry, school teachers, builders and accountants.[10] It really works!

Step 5: Gratitude

'Thank you.' Two words that can make a world of difference for both the giver and the receiver. When we take the time to feel grateful, to appreciate things and to express that feeling of appreciation in some way, life seems to be better. We resonate with the world instead of fighting with it. We notice beauty. The world seems different—better. It's hard to be depressed when you are feeling grateful.

Gratitude is a state of thankfulness and appreciation. Appreciating something involves taking the time to notice it and then acknowledging its value and meaning, as well as feeling a positive emotional connection to it. Paradoxically, in our consumer society with its wealth and material comforts, the expression of genuine gratitude can be quite hard for many of us—partly because we have grown accustomed to on-demand instant gratification, or the quick fix. Materialistic striving—the hedonic treadmill—is strongly associated with life dissatisfaction and unhappiness. Expressions of gratitude have the potential to reduce materialistic strivings and, through doing so, may reduce the negative impact of materialistic strivings on our levels of life satisfaction.[1]

The word *gratitude* stems from the Latin word *gratia*, which means grace, graciousness—to do with the kindness, generosity and appreciation of the beauty of giving and receiving—attributes that can easily be squeezed out of our time-poor contemporary lives.

Gratitude as a foundation

The idea that the cultivation and expression of gratitude is an essential foundation for a happy and virtuous life is found throughout history in the world's religions and spiritual traditions. The Buddhist, Hindu, Muslim, Christian and Jewish traditions all value gratitude.

Most of these religions have annual thanksgiving celebrations, many of which have their origins in harvest festivals.

But are traditional celebrations of gratitude merely moral imperatives—religious hangovers—or superstitious rituals? Some might think that is the case, but science shows that gratitude has some very clear benefits.

Healthy gratitude

Gratitude is associated with happiness. Gratitude as both an emotional state and an attitude towards life is a significant source of human strength.

Not only does feeling grateful improve life satisfaction in general but also grateful thinking can be a very useful way of lifting your mood.[2] In fact gratitude has a more powerful effect on well-being than personality, and has strong connections to personal growth, a purpose in life, and self-acceptance and positive relationships with others.[3]

Relationships are important. One of our basic human needs is to be appreciated and valued, to be held in positive regard. Expressions of gratitude foster the development of positive relationships. In one interesting study of college students during a week of gift-giving from older college members to new members, it was found that the expressed gratitude of the gift-receivers significantly predicted future positive relationship outcomes. Gratitude seems to be an important social lubricant.[4]

Gratitude evolves

Gratitude might well have evolutionary value. People feel grateful when they have benefited from someone who has expended intentional effort on their behalf. The experience of gratitude often motivates the beneficiaries to repay their benefactors. The beneficiaries might even extend generosity to others—when we feel grateful we are more likely to perform acts of kindness to others, and such acts in turn can create further acts of generosity and kindness. What's more, the altruistic effect of gratitude seems to be more than a simple response to feeling good about receiving something, and this seems to be a cross-cultural finding. For example, Chinese researchers looked to see whether receiving a specific and purposeful favour from someone would encourage pro-social behaviour more than just receiving a gift by chance alone. They found that people receiving a favour helped more and reported more gratitude compared to participants in the chance condition.[5]

Evolutionary theorists argue that this kind of positive reciprocity plays a unique role in human social evolution.[6] Think of the last time when someone took the time to express genuine gratitude to you for something that you had done. How did you feel? Odds are that you felt valued and appreciated. Chances are that you felt more inclined to repeat that action. Compare that memory with a time when you put a lot of time and effort into helping someone or doing something for them, and they just took it for granted. No offer of thanks. No acknowledgment. No sense that all your hard work was appreciated or even noticed. How did you feel then? Did you feel more or less willing to repeat that? Gratitude counts in relationships.

The consequences of gratitude

Robert A. Emmons from the University of California, Davis, and colleagues are engaged in a long-term research project on the nature of gratitude and its potential consequences for human health and well-being. They have found plenty of evidence to support the kinds of gratitude positive interventions suggested in this crucial step of the happiness program.

In one series of three studies they asked people to focus regularly on their blessings and to keep a gratitude journal.*

The first study asked students to keep a weekly journal. They were told to think back over the past week and write down five things in their life for which they were grateful or thankful. The sort of things the participants cited were 'waking up this morning', 'the generosity of friends', 'to God for giving me determination', 'for wonderful parents', 'to the Lord for just another day' and 'to the Rolling Stones'. A control group was told to list hassles—things that had bothered or annoyed them. They came up with things like 'hard to find parking', 'messy kitchen no one will clean', 'finances depleting quickly' and 'doing a favour for a friend who didn't appreciate it'. The gratitude group felt better about their lives as a whole, and was more optimistic about the forthcoming week than their 'hassle' counterparts.

The second study was similar in most respects except that the diaries were kept on a daily basis for two weeks. An additional control group was added. These students were asked to think about ways in which they were better off than others, and to list those. Again the gratitude group enjoyed a boost in mood and optimism, but also they were more likely to have offered emotional support to someone else or to have helped someone with a personal problem.

The third study set out to see whether gratitude could help people with chronic illness feel better. Adults with neuromuscular disease were asked to keep a daily record of their blessings for three weeks. Compared to the controls they reported higher levels of positive mood, greater optimism and a greater sense of feeling connected to others. They also slept better. Those closest to them confirmed these reports.

More recently Emmons and his collaborators have been working with young people and are finding that being grateful can help young people experience long-lasting boosts to their well-being. Two hundred and twenty-one early adolescents were randomly assigned to either counting blessings or writing about the hassles they had in life. As with the previous studies, counting blessings led to increased gratitude and enhanced well-being.[†] Those who practised gratitude were also more alert, enthusiastic, determined, attentive and energised compared to those who considered themselves better off than others but did not actively make a point of being grateful for it. They have also shown that children who practice grateful thinking have more positive attitudes towards their school and their families.

* Emmons, R.A. & McCullough, M.E., 'Counting blessings versus burdens: An experimental investigation of gratitude and subjective well-being in daily life', *Journal of Personality and Social Psychology*, vol. 84, 2003, pp. 377–89.

† Froh, J.J., Sefick, W.J. & Emmons, R.A., 'Counting blessings in early adolescents: An experimental study of gratitude and subjective well-being', *Journal of School Psychology*, vol. 46, 2008, pp. 213–33.

The positive effects of gratitude seem to be universal. Although much of the research has been conducted in the United States, the positive relationship between gratitude, happiness, psychological well-being and a wide range of character strengths has been found in wide range of cultures including the United Kingdom, Croatia,[7] Japan,[8] Thailand[9] and China. In a study of the character strengths of fifty-four nations, gratitude was one of the strengths that was consistently high across all nations.[10] It seems that we can all benefit from gratitude and appreciation.

Benefits of gratitude

The effects of gratitude show up in the most unexpected places. One study looked to see whether individual differences in gratitude were related to sleep quality. Gratitude predicted greater subjective sleep quality and sleep duration, and also predicted less dysfunctional daytime sleeping.[11] The effect of gratitude on sleep was even stronger than the effect of such personality traits as neuroticism.

Grateful customers are good for business.[12] Customers take particular notice of salespeople's generosity. Customers apparently take account of a wide range of factors when judging the service they receive. They look at the perceived risk of a salesperson's generosity; that is, what it was costing the salesperson to be generous, whether this was normal behaviour, and how genuine the act was. All of these factors influenced the level of the customer's gratitude. As the levels of gratitude rose, so did a wide range of other factors, including purchasing intentions, customer loyalty and actual purchases.

Appreciative attentional muscles?

In many ways gratitude is a skill. For those of us who weren't born grateful, gratitude is something we have to work at developing. This is particularly the case for people who are prone to depression and anxiety. We need to build our appreciative attentional muscles, to apply ourselves purposefully to making small positive changes in our lives. The mind is like a muscle. The more we use it, the more we practise specific mental exercises, the stronger our 'mind muscles' become. A simple and highly effective way is to practise the 'three good things' exercise.

One four-week randomised controlled experimental study examined the positive emotion and well-being outcomes of eighty-two people who regularly recorded positive events in their lives. The results showed that recording happy events significantly improved participants' well-being.[13]

Three good things in life

As we discuss throughout this book, we too often cruise through life on autopilot, mindlessly moving from day to day. Complacent and comfortable in our existing mindset and behaviour patterns, we rarely stop to see how we are treating life, or how we could be making positive changes. The three good things in life exercise combines gratitude with appreciation. It's very simple. You just write down three things that went well during the course of the day and a causal explanation—why it happened—for each thing. A randomised controlled study compared the three good things in life exercise to a group of people who simply wrote about early childhood memories. The research found that effects of this exercise take some time to appear, and people in the research study did not show improvements for a month. But a month after starting the three good things exercise they had increased happiness and decreased depressive symptoms, and they stayed happier and less depressed at a three-month and a six-month follow-up.[14] Many of them found it so rewarding that they carried on doing the exercise.

For the *Making Australia Happy* volunteers there was an added joy to the exercise. Each time you return to the journal you renew your enjoyment and, as Natalia discovered, it helped her focus on the good things in her life, rather than getting dragged into thinking about the bad. In one week her list of blessings included:

- a reasonably calm day at work
- getting home safely when walking back really late the other night
- flowers growing in the garden
- a chat with the guy at the coffee shop
- the kindness of others
- fresh water in a clean glass
- a beautiful sunset of soft muted cloudy light
- seeing people in love and happy together

One way that can increase the effectiveness of the three good things exercise is to talk purposively about them. Share them with friends, workmates and family. You can even post them on Facebook or other social networking websites. You could be surprised at how effective this simple exercise is at increasing your levels of well-being.

Try sharing your three good things with your family. You can do this at a family meal, in casual conversation or at any point in the day. Some people find purposefully doing this with their family quite challenging as it often breaks the usual well-established conversation patterns. It is strange, but we often are reluctant to talk about the good things in life, even in our families.

Dr Tony thought that Stephen and his family might really benefit from the exercise of sharing three good things together. Like so many families, they were caught up with what wasn't working rather than what was. Stephen was in a constant state of guilt due to getting home from work late, and his tension and guilt did not make for an ideal family atmosphere.

Dr Tony joined them for supper one evening to introduce them to the concept of three good things. 'They can be really small things,' he told them. 'It can be appreciating the beauty of the day. It could be that you've gone on a walk, or you've played a great game of football. It could be a nice meal you've shared. Or they could be very big things. But the important thing is that they are things that you feel gratitude for, that when you step back, you say, "Yes, that was really good."'

Stephen's son Ben was first up with his three good things: 'I was in school today and I didn't have any homework for three periods so that was good, and so I went down to the park, which I like doing a lot. And Dad came home early today, and that was good, and we ate dinner together for once, and that was good.'

Stephen saw immediately how the exercise would enrich his perception of daily life. 'So often I struggle to remember what I did all day, but this way the thought will be in my mind to hold on to those moments, and it will be a good way of adjusting my mindset to be more open to the positive things that are going to happen rather than getting bogged down in the problems that I spend all day solving.'

It seems that expressions of gratitude have important positive effects in a wide range of areas: health, happiness and even business. But expression of gratitude need to heard by someone, and graciously accepting expressions of gratitude and appreciation from other people might not always be easy.

'It was nothing—don't mention it'

Although we might find it relatively easy to express our gratitude to others, many of us find it hard to receive expressions of gratitude and application. We become embarrassed. We dismiss the appreciative comment with a throw-away line: 'It was nothing—don't mention it.'

Being recognised and appreciated is uncomfortable for many of us. We feel under pressure, in the spotlight, embarrassed. In order to escape these uncomfortable feelings we summarily dismiss the comments and try to move on.

But in doing so we effectively rob the other person of their opportunity to give us a gift: the gift of gratitude. Even if from our own perspective we might see the act we performed for them as being small or insignificant, we cannot really know what effect it had on them. Gracefully receiving gratitude, accepting appreciative comments, is not so much about us; it is far more about them.

Gracefully receiving appreciative comments can have a positive influence on us personally, especially where we have created something but find it difficult to accept ourselves as creative individuals. This is often the situation for many artists who are, surprisingly, often quite embarrassed by compliments about their art. Strangely, creative people might feel more comfortable with criticism than praise. Learning to accept praise from others gracefully is a useful personal development tool. But accepting praise, by allowing ourselves to be open to appreciative comments, we are in effect learning to accept ourselves. Such acceptance need not be more than a simple 'Thank you. I appreciate your positive comments'.

Cade found it very difficult to accept appreciation about his artwork. He struggled to see value or quality in his art despite the fact that he was posting it online and getting good feedback.

'I get awkward being given compliments by my friends, let alone people I have never met,' he told Dr Tony, 'and also I'm worried that they'll think I'm smug.' Dr Tony coached Cade to consider praise and appreciation as a gift that others were giving him in return for the gift of art that he had given them. Cade understood that accepting praise was about letting others know that you appreciate them.

On the night of his art show he was able to accept positive, appreciative comments, which helped him see himself as an artist and value his own work.

Looking for faults or benefits

Despite the obvious benefits of holding a grateful and appreciative attitude towards life, from time to time we become sucked into an ungrateful and deprecating frame of mind. For many people, this bleak, fault-finding mindset sometimes just seems to take them over once in a while. For other people this is like an automatic default mindset—they just seem to focus naturally on the negative.

Fault-finding is a marvellous way to spoil your day, and to spoil the days of those around you. Most of us will have had days when we just seemed to be automatically tuned in to what was going wrong. No matter what was actually said to us, what we heard was sarcasm, snippy remarks and ill-intent at the core of the message. This could be particularly true for those in long-term work or personal relationships. When we don't deal with our resentments, and the toxic legacy of resentment builds up over time, we seem to find fault easily wherever we look, particularly with those we know really well: they didn't take our opinion into account. We felt as if we were treated disrespectfully or ignored. In retaliation we started to look for where they were wrong. We watched all their actions carefully, anticipating then finding faults, inadequacies, errors. Yes— joy of joys: we proved to ourselves that we were right and they were wrong. Vindicated! Our resentments thus justified, we sought then found even more examples of faults.

Contrast this with benefit-finding. Benefit-finding is the act of look-ing for positive changes that have occurred as a result of difficult or challenging life events such as illness, accidents or other distressing life events. Not surprisingly, the research shows that benefit-finding is clearly associated with positive increases in well-being.[15] We can find benefits in even the most difficult and painful life events. Quite frequently people who are facing great difficulties such as major illness or trauma come to terms with their illness by focusing on the positive changes that have occurred as a result. This re-evaluation of the meaning of life events is not about putting on a happy face or denial. Benefit-finding is not about saying to people who are suffering, 'Just think positive and the pain will go away', or 'Be just positive and life will be easy'. Rather it is about making a choice about how we view our life situation.

In one study, cancer patients who were randomly assigned to benefit-finding—writing about the benefits of their cancer experience—had fewer subsequent medical appointments for cancer-related problems than those who wrote about the facts of their illness.[16] Benefit-finding following a heart attack reduces the risk of a subsequent heart attack. It can even reduce the risk of AIDS-related mortality for HIV-positive individuals.[17] Benefit-finding works by reducing levels of activity in our stress response system, changing our perceptions of future stressors, and increasing our ability to develop constructive ways of coping. This all helps us to define the goals we want, then focus on them, rather than feeling overwhelmed and out of control.[18]

Benefit-finding is about looking for things to appreciate and to be grateful for, even in the midst of adversity. Just as fault-finding leads us to notice ever more faults, problems and difficulties, benefit-finding helps us build our gratitude levels.

The gratitude letter and visit

As you count your blessings and benefits, you might well recognise that there are particular people to whom you are grateful. Expressing gratitude by writing a gratitude letter to them is another proven way to make you feel happier. Well-known positive psychologists Martin Seligman, Tracey Steen, Nansook Park and Chris Peterson found that people who wrote a gratitude letter to someone they had never properly thanked were happier and less depressed a month later than those who had simply written about an early memory, and the benefits lasted for up to three months.[19] Chris Peterson recommends that you read the letter aloud to the person you are thanking and that, if you do this, you will see a measurable improvement in your mood and well-being.[20] In fact it has been said that the gratitude visit is one of the most powerful exercises in Positive Psychology.

Guidelines for a gratitude letter and visit

You can write the letter any way you like. It is recommended that you actually read it aloud face to face to the person if possible, or alternatively you could visit them face to face then hand them the letter to read themselves while you stand there. If personal delivery in a 'gratitude visit' is not possible, you could post, fax or email the letter. You might then follow up by making a phone call.

If for some reason those options are not possible you might like to read it aloud as if they were listening. You might like to do this at a special place or location, one that has strong memories for you. Some people have found this to be a very useful way of expressing their gratitude to a parent, partner or friend who has passed away.

This was what Liz decided to do. She and her mother were always very close, and Liz continues to be upset by the fact that her mother died before her own children were born, partly because her mother will never know the children, but especially because, since having had children, she has even more appreciation of her own mother. Yet Liz never had the opportunity to tell her how much she appreciated her.

> I'm writing a gratitude letter to my mum [she wrote in her journal], even though my mum passed away nine years ago now ... I never got a chance to connect with her on that mother-to-mother level because she died the year before I had my first baby. Now as a parent I really am very grateful and appreciative of the kind of mother she was because so much of her parenting comes out in what I do with my kids. If they feel about me even half of what I feel about my mum I'll be more than happy.

Liz decided that the best place to read the letter to her mum was in the house where she grew up. The house had seen better times, but it still looked very familiar. She began reading:

Dear Bubs [in the last ten years of her life we called her Bubs],

I miss you every day. I never got to tell you what a fantastic mother you were because you died before I had my own babies. You made me who I am today and I'm so grateful for the person you brought me up to be. I saw you being kind to people from all walks of life. You were never rude. You always made time for everyone. You gave to charities. You loved animals. And I learnt all of this from you and I like it.

I'm grateful for the manners you instilled in us. As I'm now passing them on to my two children. Sometimes people look at me funny for trying to tell a three-year-old that they need to eat with their mouths closed or they need to hold their cutlery properly, but watching them develop these manners over the years is such a testament to your mothering because that's what you taught us to be. Even though you're 45 years older than I was, age doesn't make you any closer or further apart from somebody. If you click, you just click. And we did click. The fact that your mothering skills were so broad made it hard to pinpoint exactly what to thank you for. There's just so much. I guess watching you be such a nice person and so kind is what I feel I generally became thanks to you. I feel that I'm a good mother just like you were, and I can't be any more grateful for anything.

You weren't just my mum. You taught me all about being a mum without realising it. I see you coming out in my mothering all the time, and it makes me so proud. I can't think of anything more satisfying than to be the mother that you were. I hope my kids will talk and laugh with me the way I did with you. And I love you now just as much as I did when you were still with me.

I miss you. And I wish I still I had you on earth but I know you're near. I know that you're hearing me now and I also see you coming out in my children through their various characteristics, which I love. If I could have my time over with you now, I would love nothing more than to have coffee at our favourite little coffee shop in the Mall. Except this time it would be me, you and the kids. One day we'll be together again.

It was the first time Liz had put all these thoughts together on paper. Despite the fact that she missed her mum so much, writing it and reading it aloud did not make her sad. On the contrary it made her feel happy and positive. 'There's something solid and comforting about the fact that I've put all those thoughts and feelings down on paper and actually read it out loud.'

Some people find it helpful to keep the letter for a period (say, a week) and read it every day for that time. You might find it helpful to write about the following things:

1 Why you are writing this letter.
2 What you are grateful for. Be as specific as possible.
3 Describe the things you are grateful for in concrete terms.
4 Describe how their behaviour affected you. How you benefited. What you learnt.
5 Allow yourself to be in touch with the feeling of gratitude as you write.
6 Read and re-read the letter to ensure that it captures your thoughts and feelings.
7 Set a time and day to go on your 'Gratitude Visit'.
8 Make the visit (for many people this is the hardest part, but it is also the most beneficial).

The gratitude letter is often a challenging exercise. It can be extremely emotional. The effects can be quite powerful, both for the writer and for the recipient. But the results can also be quite surprising.

Stephen chose to thank his father. 'He's done a lot for me and been a role model for me … and I've never really properly thanked or acknowledged him for it … It's pretty difficult to tell people how you feel about them, or it is for me, so this exercise is somewhat challenging.'

Stephen had felt quite moved while he was writing the letter so he was hugely disappointed in himself that when it came to the actual reading of it, it fell flat. 'I was trying to express to my dad how grateful I am for the things he taught me, and one of those things was that showing your emotions is a strength not a weakness.' Despite the power of his feelings, Stephen showed no emotion. 'So I feel that I have let him down rather.' But on reflection he thought that the exercise had been hugely valuable in highlighting the one big area that he had to keep working on. 'I want to be as good a role model for my children as Dad was to me, and that means not being scared to show my emotions. And I realise it is going to take time and practice but that is what I am striving for.'

Remember, though, the letter is not just an 'I want to feel good' exercise. It is about expressing our thankfulness and appreciation to someone else. Ultimately, it is not about us—it's about them. Incidentally, despite any shortcomings in Stephen's delivery of the letter, his father, Tom, was absolutely delighted and deeply touched. 'Hearing Stephen read that letter to me is something that I really cherish. It will stay with me for the rest of my life.'

The reality of writing the gratitude letter then delivering it might be quite different from your expectations, so it is very important to write the letter and to deliver it without any rigid expectations of how it will be received, or what your own response will be. Express your gratitude without expecting to feel better. Do it simply for the reason that you believe that expressing your gratitude is the right thing to do.

And in the course of your day, within the fabric of your life, take time to pause and appreciate what others do for you. Express your gratitude. Take the time to say 'thank you'—two words that can really make a world of difference.

Step 6: Forgiveness

What's the worst thing anyone has ever done to you? Perhaps you were bullied at school? Maybe you've been undermined at work? Or your spouse walked out on you without warning? You might have been the victim of a horrible crime. Almost all of us have experienced being unceremoniously dumped by a boyfriend or girlfriend. Many of us will have worked for an abusive or aggressive boss.

Are you resentful? Bearing a grudge? A quick check of some newspaper headlines over the last couple of months would suggest that plenty of people are: 'I will never forgive him for what he has done to my little sister,' says the brother of a young wife dumped by her philandering footballer husband. 'I will never forgive him for his cruelty and the manner in which he decided to dispose of me,' says a TV presenter of her former boss. 'I will never forgive the pair for what happened,' says the mother of a young woman murdered by a couple of teenagers.

You might think it impossible to forgive deep-seated hurts and insults, yet the remarkable thing is that people do, and when they do their physical and mental health is the better for it.[1] Forgiveness is one of the hardest things you'll ever do, yet the remarkable thing is that many people learn to do it even when they first deemed it completely impossible and out of the question.

In this step you are going to identify a hurt or a grudge that you have been hanging on to. You are going to learn to forgive that person and move on. But first we need to understand the process of forgiveness.

Forgiveness is not about condoning, forgetting, denying or excusing the actions of the perpetrator.[2] True forgiveness rests on being able to view the offender with compassion. It requires a significant shift in perspective. It begins with recognising one's resentments, then being able to let them go. This is not easy, particularly where the resentment is longstanding and personal. Yet resentments are poison to our spirit, a cancer of the soul.

Resentments that are unfettered and unchecked manifest in our lives by clouding our judgement, disturbing us emotionally, physically and mentally, and frequently triggering self-defeating behaviour patterns.[3] They disempower us by placing us in the victim role. They trap us in the past and are a significant barrier to our enjoying the present and fulfilling our potential for happiness. Worst of all, if we do not take the time for an emotional inventory, to take stock of how we truly think and feel, we might be unaware of its destructive toll on our body and mind.

Of course it is easy to forgive things that are not deeply painful or where our resentment is not deep-seated, and practising an attitude of forgiveness on a daily basis is an important tool in our well-being and happiness toolbox. But deep-seated resentments are not like that. They are not so easily dismissed. They return to haunt us in the dead of night. We wake from sleep boiling with anger about the way we were treated or what someone said. In the midst of an enjoyable day our peace of mind is hijacked by thoughts of outrage. Our view of the world is sullied. We plot revenge. We seek humiliation of the perpetrator, getting even, getting our own back, and making them pay. Perversely, we might even find ourselves enjoying our resentments. After all, resentments can be a very useful way of distracting ourselves from making real change! And the best thing about resentments is that they make us 'right' and the other person 'wrong'.

Resentments have not been discussed much in the Positive Psychology literature. Some Positive Psychology proponents seem to shy away from the painful aspects of our lives, mistakenly promoting a simplistic smiley-happy approach to life. Yet before we can truly forgive we need to understand how the resentment process works. How many times have we thought 'I'm over that' or 'I forgive them', only to find that the resentment resurfaces again and again?

To really practise forgiveness, to let go of the resentments that bind us, we need to understand how resentment controls our outlook and our behaviour. We need to understand how our thinking patterns become resentful rumination. Once we understand the nature of resentment we can learn to forgive.

Rebekah and Natalia were so hard-wired by deep-seated resentment that they viewed themselves and the world through a filter of bitterness and hostility.

Rebekah was halfway through the series before she finally confronted that reality. She was faced with a choice: either infect her own family with the legacy of an unhappy childhood by reiterating the old hurts, or change the story. But she was scared of change. It is not simple or straightforward to give up feelings that one has become so attached to even if you might not like those feelings or the kind of person they make you become.

Natalia was so scarred by the hurt that had been inflicted upon her that it shaped the way she thought about everything—from how she felt about her body to what her marriage prospects were likely to be.

There are two key parts of the resentment process: rehearsing the hurt and harbouring a grudge.[4]

Rehearsing the hurt

Once we have been hurt and the seed of resentment has been sown, we often rehearse the hurt. In our minds we replay the story over and over again, ruminating, thinking, and feeling it again and again. We might try to undo the actions mentally, trying to make it better.

We might imagine ourselves doing or saying something that would have made a difference. We might mentally view the actions from different perspectives. Each time we do this we experience important and very real physiological changes.[5] Our blood pressure increases, our heart rate soars, emotions become aroused, the mental images get more vivid.

With each rehearsal of hurt we are ever more deeply embedding the 'I am a victim' story about the event.[6] In effect we are training our brains to recall and relive the event. Over time we might even begin to lose control over our thinking, with thoughts, feelings and images of the hurt perpetually popping into our life. We might even start to experience a post-traumatic stress disorder—not unlike the recurrent anxiety attacks people have after suffering a trauma.

Harbouring a grudge

Along with rehearsing the hurt we also tend to harbour a grudge associated with the resentment. A harbour is a place of shelter, a refuge. To harbour something means that we provide a home for it. We keep it safe. We nurture it. A grudge is a feeling of bitterness, of anger or indignation. To hold a grudge is to foster ill-will. The reality is that by harbouring a grudge we are creating a home for negative feelings inside ourselves, adding to the poison cocktail that is already destroying part of us.

Resentments affect us physically and emotionally. Resentment is associated with increased blood pressure, heart disease, increased cortisol levels and neurological changes in brain structure.[7] We literally become hard-wired for anger. We feel stressed and depressed. We ruminate, become begrudging, hostile and bitter. Often resentment towards another person turns into self-resentment over time.

In this section we are going to look at Rebekah and Natalia's stories in some depth because they both have much to tell us about the process of coming to terms with past resentment and moving towards forgiveness.

Rebekah's story

'I want to make the distinction between my family now and my family of origin—the family I grew up with as a child—because that's really important. There's this systemic loathing. It started with my mother. She just didn't have the capacity or the skills to actually teach her kids how to have fair and loving relationships, warts and all.

'I feel like I'm continually blamed for stuff by my family of origin, that I'm this bad person, that I've done all these bad things. And when I ask someone, "What actually is that?" no one can tell me. In fact no one has ever acknowledged anything in my life, good or bad. My mother has never even acknowledged the birth of my children.

'I don't want to keep banging on about the hurt, but I feel like it's never been heard. And I feel like any time I try and say anything within my family of origin, I'm told to shut up.

'My mother tries to create dysfunction within the family group. My mother complains about everyone and everything. And about me. And I live with it. Every day, all it takes is someone to mention their family, their mother or brother or their sister and I'm back there.

'I think that is the most selfish thing that my family has ever done, to not provide a safe place of unconditional love. Because they don't know how to, they've never known how to do it for themselves or each other. So that there's nowhere for me to go for some non-judgemental advice when I want to discuss issues arising in my own family.'

This is the thing about resentments. They have a really strong negative psychological influence on us. This is very well documented. Increased stress and increased anger lead to exhaustion. We feel drained. The anger spills out into other areas of our lives, undermining our capacity to deal with things.

But most damaging for Rebekah—and she knew it—was that she herself had fallen into the trap of adopting the very behaviour patterns she so despised.

'It's scary. Even though I am not an absent parent, I am aware that I'm in danger of getting caught up in the old stories and becoming an absent parent to my children. I want to find a way to stop doing this because I realise how damaging it is. The trouble is it's so ingrained, it's actually at a molecular level, because that's all I've known and all I've practised. That's part of my make-up. This is what I am familiar with.'

This aspect of being hard-wired resonated with Natalia, who felt that her hurt feelings had become so entrenched that they were part of who she was. She was not necessarily comfortable with that person, but she was used to being that way, and not sure whether she could or should change.

Natalia's story

'I had a friendship which ended abruptly after fifteen years. Not only that, my friend went to great lengths to be extremely and intentionally hurtful, and that still upsets me a lot. She made accusations and just refused to answer any of my calls. Then out of the blue came a typed letter. She had once said that the height of rudeness to a close friend is to type a letter, so she'd gone to the trouble to type this letter to make it even nastier. And it was nasty. The things she said were just awful.

'A lot of the things that really play on my mind were planted in that letter. They were my own insecurities anyway. And she knew me well enough to know that. That is almost seven years ago. Now when I'm doing a stocktake of my life and realising it's not quite what I might want it to be, I remember that letter and I think she was right, and that's frightening and very unpleasant.'

When pressed to think about what was going on in the life of the friend that would have motivated her to write such a letter, Natalia continued, 'She was probably feeling pretty scared. She was newly separated and in the frightening position of finding herself as a single mum with two young kids, and not having support.'

The friend's behaviour could be understood in such a context. It sounded as if she had lashed out like a child who strikes out at the

The power of forgiveness

Evidence is growing that people who forgive past wrongs done to them are substantially less angry, more optimistic and in better health than those who refuse to forgive and forget.[*] One powerful example is a study that offered forgiveness therapy to a group of women who had suffered emotional abuse in marriage.[†] Over a number of months they were encouraged to follow a four-step forgiveness process currently being tested in treatment and research: first, to examine the injustice of the abuse and consider forgiveness as an option; second, to make the decision to forgive. Then the hard work of forgiving: grieving the pain from the injustice, relinquishing resentment and developing goodwill; ultimately finding meaning in the unjust suffering, and discovering psychological release and new purpose.

Over the same period a second group received an alternative therapy specifically recommended for emotionally abused women. It makes room for grief but focuses on anger validation, assertiveness and interpersonal relationship skills. The forgiveness group experienced significantly greater improvement than the other in follow-up testing for depression, anxiety and post-traumatic stress symptoms.

Resentment is associated with increased blood pressure, heart disease, increased cortisol levels and neurological changes in brain structure.[‡] Several studies show that forgiveness appears to reverse that condition. One such study required seventy people to revisit hurtful memories.[§] They were asked first to go through the motions of rehashing old resentments and grudges, then to cultivate an empathetic response and to imagine themselves granting forgiveness to the person who had hurt them in real life. As expected, the unforgiving thoughts prompted muscle tension, increased sweating, quickened heart beat and raised blood pressure that persisted for some time; whereas thinking about forgiving reduced the pressure responses across the board.

In the not too distant future scientists believe they might be able to demonstrate how forgiveness has such a profound physiological effect on our nervous system. We know that revisiting resentments and going over the old stories tells the part of the brain that remembers and processes emotions to send out stress hormones. It's likely that the process of forgiveness changes the neurological sequences, so that those stress signals are disrupted or suppressed.

[*] Konstam, V., Marx, F., Schurer, J. et al., 'Forgiving: What mental health counselors are telling us', *Journal of Mental Health Counseling*, vol. 22, 2000, pp. 253–67.

[†] Reed, G. & Enright, R., 'The effects of forgiveness therapy on depression, anxiety, and post-traumatic stress for women after spousal emotional abuse', *Journal of Consulting and Clinical Psychology*, vol. 74, 2006, pp. 920–9.

[‡] Clark, A., 'Forgiveness: A neurological model', *Medical Hypotheses*, vol. 64, 2005, pp. 649–54.

[§] van Oyen Witvliet, C., Ludwig, T.E. & Vander Lann, K.L., 'Granting forgiveness or harboring grudges: Implications for emotion, physiology, and health', *Psychological Science*, vol. 12, 2001, pp. 117–23.

very person they love the most or they're closest to. 'I hate you. Go away!' And what they mean is 'hug me'. But that is not to suggest that Natalia should feel responsible or guilty. It in no way absolves the friend of responsibility for what she did. But understanding is the beginning of the process of empathy.

Forgiveness

So how do we practise forgiveness? Most of us will just try to 'forgive and forget', hoping that the hurt will go away. Unfortunately, this rarely works. Forgiveness is about making a conscious decision to adopt an attitude of compassion towards someone who has hurt us. It is a process. For many people it takes a considerable amount of time and repeated effort.

It is also about moving away from the 'story' that we have created about us being 'the victim'.

Every time we rehash the hurt, either in our own head or telling our friends about this terrible thing that someone did to us, we embed our victim story ever more firmly in our psyche. If our friends egg us on by encouraging us to dwell on our anger and seek revenge of some kind, we are likely to be stuck indefinitely in the helpless victim groove.

But you have a choice. Imagine changing the story. Instead of being the victim, in this new story you come out of it as the strong person, in control of your own destiny. However rude, unkind or cruel the wrong you suffered, you can move on.

There are several scientifically validated programs that teach the process of forgiveness. One of the best known and most frequently used by professional counsellors is the REACH program.[8] REACH is a an acronym that stands for the following:

- Recall the hurt.
- Empathise with the one who hurt you.
- Altruistic, the gift of forgiveness that you offer.

- Commitment, yours, that you make to forgive.
- Hold on to the forgiveness.
  Here's how it works.

Guidelines for a forgiveness process

1 *Recall the hurt.* If you feel overwhelmed with feelings of fear and anger, use the mindfulness skills and exercises that you have learnt to relax, but don't block out the event. Recall it fully, but as you do so begin to think about different aspects of the story. If it is really traumatic, do this in the company of a friend or a therapist.

2 *Empathise with the person.* This is the hard part of forgiveness. Have compassion for the offender. As you think about the wrong that person did to you, try to understand what their motive might have been. What factors in that person's life might have led them to act as they did? Can you begin to contemplate the notion of taking some of the responsibility for what happened? Even if you can't, at the very least you can recognise that, however awful the offence, humans are all fallible. So although you don't condone what they did, you have compassion for them.

3 *Altruistic gift of forgiveness.* As we have already learned, giving makes us feel good, whether it's twenty dollars to a stranger or doing voluntary work for the community. For you to achieve the benefit from this act of forgiveness, it must be the real thing. A true gift. Freely given. This is not as a bargaining tool merely to get rid of bad feelings. We have to let them go by feeling true empathy. True compassion. As we let go we are no longer the hostile, embittered victim. The story has changed.

4 *Commit yourself to forgiving publicly.* Sharing your forgiveness makes it more 'real', and harder to step away from. One powerful way to do this is to write a letter to the offender.

5 *Hold on!* If the old hurtful vengeful feelings return, recognise them for what they are, and use these techniques to deal with them and to let go again.

Writing a forgiveness letter

You can write the letter any way you like, but the letter is not for posting. You might choose to destroy the letter once you have written and read it out aloud, or you might choose to keep it. Some people find it helpful to keep it for a period (say, a week) and read it every day for that time. You might find it helpful to write about the following things:

1 Why you are writing this letter.
2 What you are resentful about. Be specific.
3 How their behaviour affected you.
4 How you understand their point of view, or why they did what they did.
5 What your role in maintaining the resentment is.
6 Your expression of forgiveness.
7 What it is that you appreciate about them, and an expression of your good wishes for them in the future.

You'll know it's worked if you feel that a huge weight has been lifted from you. However, forgiveness is rarely a one-off event. Resentments might well resurface.

We asked Rebekah and Natalia to write letters of forgiveness. What follows is an edited transcript of their letters and their feelings about writing them.

Natalia wrote:

I'm writing this letter to let go of the negative feelings I hold towards you … What hurts me about your behaviour the most was that you refused to talk it over with me … you used all my insecurities to cut as close to the bone as you possibly could.

The impact upon me has been great, particularly in relation to my capacity to trust other people, and it's thrown into question my belief in myself as a good friend. My self-esteem dropped badly, my feelings of security and what I could expect from others were shaken.

I'd always believed that my positive, caring behaviour towards others would be re-rewarded in return. Perhaps it's a universal truth that this isn't necessarily something that people can rely on. But with a friend who I'd been close to for fifteen years, I never dreamt I could be so badly treated.

I have harboured this ongoing resentment initially by keeping and re-reading your poison letter and letting it hurt me by taking it on board to the point where it ate at me and further fed my insecurities.

I suspect part of me didn't even want to let it go because it was all I had left of our relationship. I feel like I can understand your actions better now in hindsight, and I am ready to forgive you and let this pass. You too are only human. You were hurting terribly, and likely lashed out at me as someone close to you. I can understand that and I forgive you.

There were so many things I loved and appreciated about you, your artistic nature and love for symmetry, beauty and perfection. Your love of words and language, your mischievousness and humour. We shared some beliefs and values that shaped me greatly into the person that I am today. We had a great connection and bond over such formative years of our lives. I admire you for forging ahead into unknown and daunting territory to do what you felt was right. I hope that your life is happy and full of love. I wish you and your family the very best, now and in the future.

Natalia felt physically different after writing the letter. She was surprised that she had been able to feel empathy towards her friend with such sincerity. She felt 'lighter', as if a load had been lifted from her.

Rebekah said, 'I wrote my letter to my parents, and I really had to work hard at being empathetic. I think I got there at the end, but I was very resistant towards that and the last bit was very hard. I really had to dig down and try to find some common ground, perhaps a shared experience of being a parent.'

Rebekah's letter:

Dear Mum and Dad.

There has been great pain and suffering in my life. As part of the healing process and so that I can move forward, I've learnt that I need to forgive you so I can be free of resentment. I feel as though I have come to a brave place, although I'm scared witless. I've come to a place where I have developed a greater understanding of myself and how I work in the world.

My heart's desire is to live life well and to the full, free of the ghosts of the past generations and the memories that cloud and colour my world, keeping me stuck in the past, robbing me of my future, of its full potential and capacity to live mindfully. I'm most resentful for the lack of concern that you both had for me as a child. You were too busy and distracted with your own pain and resentments to see the impacts it had on the people around you.

Mum, your self-centredness, and Dad, your inability to connect and communicate authentically has had far reaching impacts on my life. I've fought constantly to feel accepted and loved by the world, which is an impossible feat …

I forgive you for being absent parents. Thank you for giving life to me, and in giving life to me I've given life to the two most amazing little boys in the entire universe. I'm truly thankful for the precious gift of life, this greatest gift of all. Even with its ups and downs, I love what life has given me. I know that there is a place in both of your hearts where you really do love me unconditionally.

I wish you both contentment, inner peace, fulfilment and most of all that you two can make peace with the world and all that occupy it, and find a place of unconditional love and acceptance.

Rebekah confessed that she had initially struggled with writing the letter because she was not convinced that she really wanted to let her parents ' off the hook', as she put it. This is a major turning point in forgiveness: giving up our right to revenge, giving up our right to get our own back and indeed letting the offender off the hook. But until we do, we are the ones trapped and wriggling on the end of that fish-hook. Rebekah was able to acknowledge that staying caught on the hook was scarier than missing out on how life could be once she was able to let go.

But she also realised that writing her letter had not magically wiped away her resentment. Both she and Natalia were going to have to keep working at the forgiveness process.

That is what the last part of the REACH process is all about—holding on to that sense of forgiveness—because it will go and it will come back, and the resentment will also go and come back.

Forgiveness can be a painful and slow process. It doesn't happen overnight. Resentments cloud our vision. They limit the way we can see. Forgiveness can give us a new window. A new perspective. The freedom to view ourselves and the world differently. But that window can mist up again and again. When the resentment comes back we need to get back to work. Clean the window—so we can see clearly again.

Stick with it. When you feel that resentment come back, recognise that as being caught on the hook again, and allow yourself to get off it.

Write your letter from the heart, not from the head. You might need to read and re-read the letter many times before you feel that you have sincerely let go of the resentment and truly forgiven the wrong. When you have, you might want to burn the letter. A lot of people do. It's a very powerful, symbolic way of saying goodbye.

Make no mistake—the act of forgiveness is a very difficult act, much harder than random acts of kindness or counting your blessings.

It is probably one of the hardest things that we have to do in our personal, emotional and spiritual development. However, if we're going to successfully cut the damaging ties with the past, this is an important step on the journey.

Step 7: Social networks

People need people. We need each other far more than we realise. Fundamentally we are social animals. The average person spends about 80 per cent of their waking hours with other people. People typically don't like to be alone. In one large-scale study, being alone was ranked the least positive experience when compared to spending time with customers, co-workers or even the boss.[1] Many people go to great lengths not to be alone. But being physically alone in itself is not unhealthy. Surprisingly, living alone is not generally related to poor physical or psychological health, especially for women in their sixties, who often fare better on their own than do women living with a spouse.[2] The problem is not being alone. It's loneliness.

Loneliness is the experience of being socially isolated. It is the perception of being socially isolated, the chronic subjective experience of isolation, rather than an objective distancing from others that makes the difference. People's subjective experience of being isolated is often not related to their number of actual social contacts.[3] Social contact is not the same as social connectedness—you really can be lonely in a crowd.

Loneliness really hurts

Loneliness hurts. It really hurts. Social pain is just as real as physical pain.[4] We might rationalise intellectually that any social pain we receive from other people such as rejection, rebuffs or negative responses are only subjective experiences, not like the 'real' physical pain of spraining a wrist or breaking a leg. But the brain registers social pain in the same regions as physical pain—there is a clear social–physical pain overlap in the underlying neural circuitry.[5] To the brain, pain is pain, irrespective of origin.[6]

Chronic loneliness does serious damage and is associated with a wide range of negative physical and mental health outcomes. Loneliness in adolescents and young adults predicts the number of high cardiovascular risk factors (e.g. body mass index, blood pressure, cholesterol) and depression in adulthood.[7] In adults, loneliness is

Rejection hurts

A 2003 neuroimaging study set out to demonstrate that the 'hurt' feelings that result from rebuff and rejection are much more than metaphorical. They invited a group of people to play cyber ball, a virtual ball-tossing game, while they scanned their brains in an fMRI scanner. The game was rigged. First up, they were told that due to a fault, they could only watch, not participate. Then they were allowed to participate. Initially it appeared that they were being included in the game but, after a while, no one passed them the ball. They were rejected. In fact it was not a real game but a pre-set computer program designed to see how they would be affected by being excluded.

As predicted, the brain responded in the same way as it would respond to physical pain. The anterior cingulated cortex, the neural alarm system that responds to physical pain, lit up. This happened both times when they couldn't participate. However, when they perceived that they had been deliberately excluded there was also activity in the prefrontal cortex—an area associated with regulating symptoms of physical pain.

Afterward, participants filled out questionnaires assessing their level of social distress during the time they had felt rejected. The activity in the prefrontal cortex correlated with the times when they reported feeling distressed, providing evidence that the experience and regulation of social and physical pain share a common neuroanatomical basis.[*]

[*] Eisenberger, N.I., Lieberman, M.D. & Williams, K.D., 'Does rejection hurt? An fMRI study of social exclusion', *Science*, vol. 302, 2003, pp. 290–2.

related to the progression of Alzheimer's disease, promotion of suicidal ideas and behaviour, poor sleep patterns, alcoholism, reduction in independent living, diminished immunity, depressive symptoms and ultimately mortality in older adults.[8]

Loneliness breeds loneliness

Social isolation is increasing. In the United States 80 per cent of Americans have no one outside their family to confide in, and 25 per cent report having no one to confide in at all, a figure that has doubled since 1985.[9]

In Australia 16 per cent of adults between the ages of 22 and 44 report that they often feel very lonely, with the deepest levels of loneliness being felt by women aged 75 and older and by men aged 35 to 44. Men who live alone or who are single fathers are more vulnerable to social isolation and loneliness, even if they appear to socialise with others.[10] Over time those who are vulnerable to loneliness tend to become increasingly isolated. When people feel lonely and isolated they tend to act towards other people in a more suspicious and apprehensive fashion, even showing hostility. Behaviour of this kind makes it hard for others to form friendships and relationships with them, so lonely people easily create a vicious cycle of loneliness, becoming less trusting, experiencing failed relationships, then more loneliness and a decreased sense of self-esteem and competency. They try to reach out, fail to connect, fail to make friends and end up disillusioned and even lonelier than before.

Loneliness breeds loneliness. In one large-scale study researchers noted the friendship histories of people, then looked at the relationship between friendship histories and people's levels of loneliness over time. They found that non-lonely people who hang around with lonely people tend to grow lonelier over time and lonely people tend to be moved to the edge of the social network when they become lonely. They get pushed aside, left on the fringe.[11] There is considerable stigma attached to being lonely. Lonely people are often viewed as being somehow strange, damaged or undesirable. Some lonely people are reluctant to admit that they are lonely. But we can recognise these patterns, and the patterns can be broken.

When we sent our volunteers to Marrickville shopping centre to do random acts of kindness for strangers, Ben's experience illustrated the value of social connections. Ben was struggling with feelings of awkwardness and fears of rejection, but he overcame his reluctance and went over to an older man who was sitting at a table all by himself. 'I know this is going to sound really weird,' Ben said, 'but I just want to do a random act of kindness today and I'd like to boost your happiness by giving you $20—no strings attached—to help pay for your coffee and your doughnut.' That was the beginning of a conversation that lasted for half an hour. Ben had given something more important than the money. Ben had given his time and made a connection, and they both felt far better for it.

Cade was someone who was wrapped up in his own sense of loneliness. His social anxieties made him unwilling to go out and meet others. Until he saw the impact of random acts of kindness at first hand it hadn't occurred to him that he could make himself and others feel happier by connecting with them in small ways.

'Saying hello to people in the street, or holding a door open for someone: who's it going to hurt? There will be people who are busy and just look down and don't respond. But for some people it will put a little bounce in their step. And that could pick up their whole day! People get so caught up in their day, rushing to the train, rushing to work, rushing to the grocery store. And this tiny little thing is just saying "Hi", just making contact with other people. It's just general kindness, and it can actually really have a major impact on people.'

For those who live alone, feel alone or just want to be happier, social engagement and social connectedness make a crucial difference. We need to connect, and we need to connect well, at a meaningful level. The science shows that it works.

Well-being is being well connected

As far back as 1893 social scientists noted the positive influence of personal or social networks on well-being.[12] Social networks bring people together. They provide buffers against hard times. They provide physical and mental resources and make people more resilient. They give people a sense of identity. And they give people a way to give back to others.

In one longitudinal study that started in 1965, people with more social contacts were significantly less likely to die in the following nine-year period than those with very few contacts. Being connected, being involved in social relations, has a strong positive effect on well-being even to the effect of reducing mortality.[13] But the effect of social networks is not always quite so dramatic. Networks can provide important sources of information, as well as psychological and social support. They can reduce the negative effects of unemployment, help you deal with life transitions such as going to university or moving house,[14] even help you improve at sport,[15] and the more people you have in your personal network, the more happy you tend to be.[16]

A social or personal network is a social structure made up of individuals who are connected in one way or another to other people in the network. The relationships that make these connections can include friendships, kinships, work and common interests such as sport or political activism, social or recreation interests. Social networks exist on a wide range of levels from couples and families to work groups and local communities up to the level of states, nations and beyond.

The influence of social networks is often overlooked, partly because we simply do not see them—we live and breathe within the network. We rarely see it from the outside. Like fish swimming in water or humans walking though the air, we fail to see them. But social networks exert a great deal of influence on people. As we have seen so far, perceived isolation from a social network can result in loneliness and significant distress.

We can study and analyse social networks. Social network analysis looks at the kinds of relationships between individuals in the network, as well as the way the network is structured. Social networks are often represented in the form of a map. The individual points in the network are called 'nodes' and the links between nodes are called 'ties'. Networks are typically represented graphically as in a map, showing the relevant ties as lines drawn between different nodes in the network. Using social network analysis computer software, researchers can work out how different parts of the network, or different properties of the individual nodes, affect each other. It is also possible to look at how the network changes and adapts over time and to see how individual nodes in the system affect each other.

Happiness is contagious

It seems that, just as smoking, fashions, obesity and headaches can spread from person to person, so emotions can be transferred from person to person. Think of the last time you happily walked into a room only to find a bunch of depressed, stressed or miserable people there. Odds are that your mood changed. That kind of change often happens even without our direct awareness. This kind of 'emotional contagion' works through the unconscious copying of body language, facial expressions and use of language. Even our unconscious beliefs about other people can be transmitted—we 'read' other people's minds all the time, and we are often quite accurate.[17]

The emotional contagion effect is even found between strangers. One study looked at the effect of emotions in retail banking. In studying interactions in thirty-nine US banks, the researchers found that, when bank tellers expressed positive emotions, customers were more satisfied with the bank's service and also felt happier.[18] Smiling and showing positive emotions to customers can even increase the size of tips in cafés and restaurants.[19]

So the research shows that on an individualistic basic we can positively influence each other. But can happiness be viral? Can it spread throughout a social network?

Can happiness spread throughout social networks?

One study examined the relationships between 4739 individuals using data collected over twenty years from 1983 to 2003.[20] There were a total of 53 228 ties between individuals—on average each individual had a total of 11.23 ties to others in the network through friendship, family, spouse, co-worker or neighbour relationships. Importantly for this research, there were many friendships in the network: 45 per cent of the people in the study were connected via friendship to another person. Because the data was collected at a number of different points over the twenty years, the researchers were able to track changes in the network over time.

The findings were very interesting. Happy people tended to be connected to one another. People with more friends tended to be at the centre of their network, and network analysis showed that happy people tended to be clustered together. People at the core of their local networks were more likely to be happy whereas those on the periphery were more likely to be unhappy. The researchers argued that happiness is not just a function of the individual but is a property of groups of people.

The fascinating thing was that changes in happiness over time seemed to ripple through the network, creating clusters of happy and unhappy people. The effect was found for a number of different relationships. For example, next-door neighbours who become happy tend to increase the other neighbour's chances of increasing their happiness by 34 per cent on average, and siblings who live within 1.6 kilometres and become happy increase their siblings' chances of being happy by 14 per cent on average.

Friends of happy people tended to be happy, as were the friends of the friends of the friends of happy people. A person was 15 per cent more likely to become happier if a friend becomes happy. This figure drops to 10 per cent if a friend of a friend becomes happy, and drops again to 6 per cent if a friend of a friend of a friend becomes happy. In other words, happiness spread through the network for three degrees of separation. So, although the effects of becoming happy on other people in the local areas of the network tended to be quite strong, the effect dissipates and decays before affecting the whole network. There are some limits to the spread of happiness!

Creating ripples of happiness

In *Making Australia Happy* Dr Tony challenged our volunteers to spread a little viral happiness deliberately around the Marrickville community. He asked them to host a dinner in a local restaurant. The catch was that the guests had to be strangers, or at least people in the community whom they knew by sight but did not know well. Once they had overcome their inhibitions about approaching people they hardly knew, they were emboldened to invite acquaintances they had met in the local shops and library as well as neighbours and friends.

The event was a huge success. Far from being awkward or stilted, as some had feared, conversation flowed along with the wine and food. Initially sceptical, Tony was thrilled with how it turned out. 'Good food and wine, good company and conversation, it's the apex of human communication. And this is just perfect. Everyone felt very comfortable, so yes, I think it was a good idea.'

His guest ended up enjoying herself as much as he did. 'Initially when Tony invited me,' she said, 'I thought it would be a little bit painful. But I've been really pleasantly surprised. I had a great conversation with the people at the table, particularly those that I didn't know. And it was really fun and I made some great community connections.'

At the end of the evening new networks had been forged. There was much talk of catching up again, and organising other events to which everyone would bring another different friend. Viral happiness in action!

Making changes—five rules

There seem to be five 'rules' of social networks that we need to be aware of if we are to use social networks in order to increase our well-being.[21] These are:

1 We shape our network.
2 Our network shapes us.
3 Our friends affect us.
4 Our friends' friends' friends affect us.
5 The network has a life of its own.

Social networks are rather like living breathing organisms. They are complex. They change over time. They seem to pulse with life. Each part of the system affects other parts, and the system as a whole affects the parts within it. We can be passive parts of the network system, or we can make a choice to be an active agent of change within the system.

We can shape our network. For example, we can exert influence over how many people we are connected to. We can choose to connect to more people. We can choose to make better quality connections. We can make new friends. Join new groups. We can introduce different people from different groups to each other. In doing so we can move ourselves more towards the centre of the network. Are you at the centre, or hanging around on the periphery? Ask yourself—how can you shape your network? If you want to increase your happiness and well-being, which is more useful: to be a wallflower or a networker?

Our network shapes us. We can make purposeful changes to the system and, in doing so, take advantage of the fact that the network in turn shapes us. By positioning ourselves more towards the centre of the network, more opportunities will come our way. In many ways the network system will support us in sustaining positive change once we start acting in a positive proactive fashion.

Our friends shape us. We tend to adopt the habits, behaviour and beliefs of those we hang out with. If your friends are heavy alcohol drinkers then the odds are that you will increase your alcohol consumption. Hang out with people who eat a lot, and you will probably start to eat more, too. What goes on around us becomes the norm, the unspoken rules by which we live our lives. You can chose to hang out with positive, happy people. You can make choices about who you are friendly with. How happy and positive are the people you currently hang out with?

Our friends' friends affect us. The influence of other people spreads through three degrees of separation. You are affected by people you don't know and have never met! How does that change the way you view friendships?

The network has a life of its own. The network is a complex and adaptive system. It adapts and changes in response to changes within it and to forces outside it. And because there are so many different possible connections between different nodes in the system, because the system can be so complex, it is often impossible to predict those changes precisely. This means that we can't completely control the outcome. We can't control, for example, how other people will react. How the friends of our friends will react. How they, in turn, will affect us. We can exert some influence. But we can't exert complete control. We can influence outcomes but not control them. Many people find the idea of not being able to control outcomes rather disconcerting. How do you react to this notion? Are you able to go with the flow, or do you need to be in control?

Useful tools for building connections

If we want to use the idea of networks in order to increase our happiness we need to make meaningful connections with other people. Some people find this very easy. Others struggle more. There are some simple but very effective tools and techniques we can use.

Be proactive: don't wait for people to come to you. Talk to other people. If you find talking to people challenging, take a course in communication skills. Join community groups. Be active in the community. Volunteer to help. Take a risk! If you meet someone you like, don't be inhibited by fear of rejection. Invite them for coffee. Alternatively, you could even host a dinner, like our volunteers.

Learn to develop rapport. Rapport is a vital part of a meaningful relationship. It is a feeling of being 'in sync' with the other person. We can all develop rapport-building skills. It's really not that hard. Put your focus totally on the other person. Use people's names. Vary the pace, rhythm and tone of your voice to keep people interested. Find out what's important to the person you are talking to. Look for common points of interest. Avoid talking about yourself.

Be a good listener. Here you can use mindful listening skills to good advantage. Think about how good it feels to be on the receiving end when somebody is really engaging with you mindfully, paying full attention to you, and compare that to how it feels when you are talking to someone and you know that their mind is wandering and they are only half listening. You can train yourself to be a good listener.

Dr Russ illustrated the power of constructive listening by getting our volunteers to sit in pairs and to practise staying mindfully present with the other person while each took turns to talk and listen. He asked the talkers to bring to mind first a very happy memory. The challenge for those listening was that they were to empathise with their partner without speaking, so they had to rely on facial expressions and gestures. They repeated the exercise, only this time recalling and speaking about a very sad personal experience.

Tony chose to tell Rebekah about his dog who had recently been diagnosed with cancer and did not have long to live. At first he found himself trying to make light of his feelings by making a few jokey asides, but as he talked he discovered the power of getting in touch with his feelings, and he became teary. But he found the experience of listening attentively to Rebekah as she talked about the death of her brother even more of an eye-opener, and resolved to put constructive listening into practice on a regular basis. 'It's taught me I should listen more. I switch off a lot when I'm not interested in the person or the conversation. I do it a lot with my wife when she's trying to tell me something, and I've got to not do that with people I care about.'

Next time someone engages you in conversation, really listen to what they are saying. Notice the language, the body language, the emotion, the facial expressions. Be mindful in your listening.

Support others. Avoid feeling competitive or jealous of others when they succeed. Celebrate their successes. Make them feel good. Remember that the happier those around you are, the happier you will be!

Keep in touch. Make sure you answer phone calls, return emails and even use social networking websites. You need to let people know that you care about them.

Respond and connect. Give back to others. If a relationship is not going the way you would like it to, make a decision to give the very thing that you want to receive. If you want respect, show respect. If you want love, be loving. Take time to express your appreciation for friends, family and co-workers. Say thank you. Show your appreciation.

Be an energiser. Put positive energy into your relationship. Don't be the person who drains the life out of a group. Avoid complaining. Avoid emotional dumping. If you want to create positive and supportive connections you need to be positive and supportive.

Finally, enjoy other people. Perhaps the most potent way of stimulating a social network is to enjoy other people. Forget about yourself and make them feel comfortable. Make them feel happy.

When it comes to social networks, what goes around really does come around.

Step 8: Reflect, review, renew

There comes a point in every journey when it's time to stop. Time to pause. To take stock and appreciate our progress. By taking the time to reflect and review, our motivation and enthusiasm becomes renewed. We deepen our learning. Re-energised, we can make new choices about how to move forward.

Let's take the time to look at what we have done so far. Let's reflect on our experiences. If you have kept notes or a journal—now is the time to go back over them. If you didn't make written notes but tried some of the steps, run over your experiences in your mind. Recall what happened. Write it down. Reflect on how far you have come. What was effective for you? What have you learnt about these steps, about happiness, about yourself?

We encourage you to keep a journal and to write about your experiences. This kind of writing is not just about keeping a priority list of things that you have to do—although writing priority lists at the beginning of the day helps us organise our thinking.[1] They reduce the amount of information we need to hold in our heads at once and can reduce stress and make us more effective.[2] To-do lists can reduce stress—but let's go beyond stress reduction.

Express yourself!

Writing about your emotions, about your life, about your life experiences—letting it all out on paper—is a very powerful way to improve your well-being. When you write in a personal, expressive fashion your mind is replaying the scenario you are writing about. You relive it. You re-experience it.

As you write, as you get into the process of expression, different thoughts, ideas and images will come to mind. Behind the scenes, while this is happening, you are allowing your unconscious mind to reorganise that information as well as a vast amount of related information. Insights surface. You make sense of your experiences. You integrate the things you are writing about into your broader life experience. You make connections. New meanings emerge. And it feels good. Recent research suggests that expressive writing is associated with increased levels of dopamine—the brain neurotransmitter associated with pleasure.[3] But be careful—some people have even speculated that expressive online writing can become addictive![4]

Of course the purpose of journalling about your experiences of this program is to help you make the most of your experience. But let's emphasise this point—writing about these experiences is therapeutic in its own right. Expressive writing and journalling can significantly deepen our learning, and can even help boost our working memory,[5] particularly if it is done over three to five consecutive days, even for just fifteen to twenty minutes at a time.[6] It works. Try it!

Four key questions

At the end of their eight weeks on *Making Australia Happy* we asked our volunteers to reflect on their experiences and we posed four key questions:

1 What have you learnt?
2 How have you changed?

3 Are you happier?

4 How do you see the future?

You might find it useful to read what some of them had to say and then ask yourself the same four questions. Use them to guide *your* reflections. Take your time. Think about your experiences. Write it out.

What have you learnt?

The program was broken down into eight steps in order to make it simple and straightforward to do. That does not mean that it is not challenging.

In step 1 we asked you to write your own eulogy. None of our volunteers found this easy. You might have found this hard, too. What was that like for you? What did you learn?

Ben told us: 'It wasn't until I had to write out that eulogy that I realised I didn't really think of the future at all very much—not to any great lengths, not to anything useful. I sort of glossed over it. I never made too many plans. That's one thing I've realised was really lacking in my life—those goals and values didn't really exist for me at all. And now I'm hell bent on not just having them but reviewing them and revaluating them and making sure they're what I want. People's minds change all the time so you need to be sure.'

We then moved on to altruism and acts of kindness—doing things for other people. We found that not only are happy people more altruistic[7] (as one might expect) but also altruism has all sorts of benefits, including improved long-term physical and mental health. Being altruistic can actually make you happier.

Stephen was surprised and delighted that something as simple as giving away chocolates in the Marrickville shopping centre could provide an instant rush of happiness, both to him and to the recipients. Quietly and unobtrusively he started to introduce random acts of kindness into his routine, little things like bringing boxes of doughnuts to his son's cricket match, giving boxes of fruit to a local boarding house, putting time into the school and community sports teams.

Liz K found the notion of deliberately committing random acts of kindness slightly artificial, yet she spent her life committing small anonymous acts of kindness for her neighbours and friends that made her feel good. 'I like that aspect of it—that nobody ever knows,' she told us.

As our volunteers found out for themselves, there is also a physical benefit from being altruistic: performing acts of altruism can boost your immune system.[8]

In step 3 we learnt about mindfulness, being present in the moment. Being in the here and now. Some of the techniques we learned included defusion—separating or detaching from our thoughts; the leaves on a stream exercise—learning to watch our thoughts drift through our minds as if they were leaves on a stream; and savouring—taking five minutes to eat just one sultana.

Liz found the mindfulness particularly powerful: 'The most valuable part for me in this eight weeks … [was] learning mindfulness … I needed to stop living in the past, stop making things up in a future you don't even know yet, just live in what you have now and enjoy what you have now … once the moment's gone you're not going to get it back!'

Liz K found that mindfulness exercises helped her be calmer: 'My sleeping patterns have improved vastly because of it. I wish I'd met mindfulness a few years ago, maybe thirty or forty years ago, because when I was younger I was a lot more frustrated, which resulted in anger and irritation. Mindfulness would have been magic to help get through that.'

Mindfulness helped Rebekah, who now understands what authentic happiness is all about: 'I was expecting a feeling like … wow, I've won the lotto but that's not what true happiness is about. It is the everyday small moments in life. Noticing the precious moments. They have always been there. But it's actually really absorbing it at a microscopic level like the joy on my kids' faces. I thought these special times and moments were really scarce but they are everyday moments. That is the mindfulness about what we have been doing and what we have been learning. It's a very quiet, still place.'

We focused on strengths and solutions in step 4. We saw how our mindset has a major influence on what we notice and how we experience the world. We learnt to cultivate a solution-focused mindset that would help us achieve our goals and fulfil our happiness potential. We learnt the power of taking small steps. We learnt how to become attuned to solutions rather than problems. How to recognise strengths in ourselves and others.

Our volunteers identified their top five character strengths and set out to use them differently. Tony discovered that gratitude was his top strength yet, until making the television series, he had not been in the habit of practising it.

Tony: 'I learnt to be grateful. When we went to the homeless shelter and we helped feed the homeless, that was a good experience for me. You go home and you say, "Look what I've got. Be grateful for what I have and what I have achieved." You tend to lose focus in life, and then you realise, "My life could be like this, but I've done quite well and I should be happy and I should do more of that." That was a good turning point for me.'

Stephen's top strength was 'judgement and open-mindedness'. This strength is about thinking things through and examining them from all sides; not jumping to conclusions; being able to change one's mind in light of evidence; and weighing all evidence fairly. He recognised that he had somehow lost sight of that trait: 'The complexity of my life had built up, I hadn't kept pace with it. I had allowed myself to get locked in to a limited way of looking at things … It's been a wake-up call to look at what is really important in my life, and to take time to look at a broad range of things rather than having tunnel vision.'

Cultivating a solutions-focused mindset and solving the big picture by taking small steps worked well for Stephen, who by the end of the series had gradually introduced regular exercise and time out with his family.

Liz also embraced this skill: 'At the beginning of the show one of the things I wanted to achieve was to try to get some kind of inner peace and calm, and I feel like I'm on my way there. I have relaxed more about life in general. Everything used to be rush, rush, rush, but now I've started to step back and not worry about being a few minutes late. One day I was in a rush to drop the kids off, but my daughter hadn't yet read to me. I had the books in my hand and went to pack them in her schoolbag. Instead I decided to sit down and read them and not worry about being a few minutes late. We had a lovely five minutes.'

For Ben it worked a treat: 'I haven't kicked a million goals, I've just started some things and I'm feeling better. It surprises me that taking small steps took very little effort … Once I got into it and realised I needed to improve my life and that a lot of things were hanging on me changing my home situation, then things started to fall into place … It makes me feel like I'm in control of my destiny once more, which I haven't felt for quite some time. And it feels like I'm an active participant in my life instead of just letting things go on around me, totally out of control. It's pretty cool.'

Step 5 was about gratitude and appreciation—getting ourselves off the frantic hedonic treadmill. Taking time to appreciate rather than consume. We saw that the positive effects of expressing gratitude were universal.[9] We found that gratitude can improve sleep[10] and can even be good for business.[11] Most importantly, even if we were not 'born grateful', gratitude is something we can purposefully develop. And taking time to notice three good things in our lives each day— being grateful—is a really effective way of boosting our happiness levels.[12]

The written gratitude exercises, particularly 'Three Good Things', really resonated for Natalia and for Ben.

Natalia: 'I think the gratitude … because it is just so easy to think something for a split second [and then] it can be gone—but if you take that time to write it down it reminds you … [Practising gratitude] keeps the scales a little more balanced rather than letting your head become overweighted with negative stuff.'

Ben: 'It affects me to look back on all the good things that are happening in my life. I feel excited just reading them actually. Doing the "Three Things" exercise hasn't yet affected my outlook on what's coming up. It's more of a retrospective look. But I think the more that I do it and the more I realise there are all these little things there—it will perk me up.'

In step 6 we learnt about letting go of resentments and practising forgiveness. For Natalia and Rebekah this was a challenging and difficult step. They both had longstanding and bitter resentments. They began their journey of coming to terms with those resentments and moving towards forgiveness by trying to empathise with the people who had hurt them and writing a letter of forgiveness to them. This was a very powerful exercise for both of them, and both recognised that it was something they would have to revisit many times.

Natalia: 'Letting go of this huge emotional angst and everything involved in this situation is something I've wanted to do for a long time, so it's really good to have seriously tackled it. I don't feel like the process is over. But I really feel I've gotten over a huge hurdle.'

Like Natalia, Rebekah felt that this was just the beginning of the process. 'It's just the start of learning how to incorporate forgiveness in my life, to ensure that those old resentments are just that—old resentments, not current. Because why should they have such presence in my life? They don't deserve to be there. I want some other room in my life for other things.'

As we all know, unfettered and unchecked resentments damage us.[13] They cloud our judgement, disturb us emotionally, physically and mentally.[14] Who needs them? Forgiveness is healing.[15] But letting go is not easy. The forgiveness letter can be a very effective way of letting go. What was your experience?

In the seventh step we connected. We saw that the loneliness of social pain is just as real as physical pain.[16] Fortunately, happiness is contagious and you can catch it. And this works both on an individual level[17] and a social level.[18] We learnt that the influence of happiness can spread through social networks. People at the core of their local networks are more likely to be happy whereas those on the periphery are more likely to be unhappy. But we can build supportive networks. We can connect. And in doing so we can increase our well-being.

Of all our volunteers Cade was the most socially isolated. He discovered that getting out and making connections made him happier than he could ever have imagined. 'For most of my life I found my shyness and my anxiety about meeting new people and social situations was almost suffocating. I used to let it prevent me from meeting new people, from attending certain events. I've learnt that the benefits of pushing through the anxiety—meeting new people, going to exciting new places—is so worth the stress that I will feel prior to it. The rewards afterwards are just amazing.'

Tony was the opposite of Cade, always outgoing and sociable. He learned to connect on another level by being more mindful in his relationships, listening more, letting others have their say. Tony: 'It's taught me patience: Relax, life's short, you know—your turn will come. That's what I've learnt, to be patient, and wait … You learned to be calm, be patient, wait your turn.'

Individual experiences

As you can see, each of the eight volunteers found that some steps were more effective for them than other steps. Each person who works through these eight steps will have a different experience. Individual personal style will make a big difference.[19] One size does not fit all. There are no 'right' experiences here—just your own personal experience.

How have you changed?

Every one of our eight volunteers felt they had changed to a greater or lesser extent.

Liz: 'My most significant change is definitely that I am not taking on negative thoughts and comments and owning them. I don't stew about things any more. I'm letting them go.'

Stephen: 'I think I've been forced to change the way I think about a lot of things. That's a real positive. I've opened myself up to a range of things I perhaps would never have chosen to do.'

Ben reported that his entire life had changed! Cade and Tony felt that their core values had not changed but that the program had drawn them out. Tony: 'I've had all these values built into me from day dot, from my parents. This program has probably just bought it back out in me … the techniques were there and it's up to you to do it.'

Change of course is a continuous process, as Natalia acknowledged. Natalia: 'I can say honestly that I'm more at ease with where I'm at. I am not giving myself a hard time about not meeting expectations that I've put in place or society has put in place. I recognise it's fine to be up and down, and that sadness and anger aren't necessarily bad. They are the natural range of human emotions; it's only right to feel them … I think I am being kinder to myself, but I haven't completely changed. I have definitely still got things to work on. I think I find it quite difficult to connect with myself emotionally and that is something that I have become more aware of and something that I intend to work on so it is good to have that goal all lined up.'

Mind–body connection

It's no good feeding your mind if you neglect to feed your body. Before our volunteers began their journey we assessed their physical fitness. Extending the motor car analogy, you could say that most

Postures of confidence

A trick to help you feel happier: sometimes it's really hard to lift your mood, however hard you try. Here's a good trick to help you feel up beat: walk tall and sit up straight. It really works!

Posture sends out powerful messages. If you sit up straight, like a newsreader, you will feel like someone with authority, confidence and credibility, and that is how you will appear to others. If you slouch and slump you will feel dejected and disengaged as well as looking that way.

The latest science shows that by adopting good posture we actually *affect* our emotions as well as reflect them. A study conducted at Ohio State University invited a number of students for a fictitious job interview.[*] They were told to fill in a questionnaire. One group was told to sit up straight, the other group to slouch. Both groups had to list three positive traits and three negative traits about themselves relating to how they would perform on the job. They found that the slouchers were less likely to believe positive things about themselves than the ones sitting up straight. So it tells us that the straighter you are, the more confident your brain becomes because it's getting the confidence messages from your body.

'Most of us were taught that sitting up straight gives a good impression to other people,' said Richard Petty, co-author of the study and a psychology professor at Ohio State University. 'But it turns out that our posture can also affect how we think about ourselves. If you sit up straight, you end up convincing yourself by the posture you're in.'

[*] Briñol, P., Petty, R.E. & Wagner, B., 'Body posture effects on self-evaluation: A self-validation approach', *European Journal of Social Psychology*, vol. 39, no. 6, 2009, pp. 1053–64.

of the Marrickville Eight were decidedly rusty, rather low on oil and with an almost empty petrol tank!

Liz and Rebekah were the only ones committed to physical exercise. Yet they were doing far too much. Always revving the engine. Cornering at high speed. Wheel spins and burnouts. They were driving their car right into the ground.

Not a single one of them was sleeping satisfactorily.

With the help of our mind–body coach Anna-Louise Bouvier, everyone developed a physical fitness program to suit their individual needs. It made a fundamental difference to the life of our most sedentary couch potato, Cade. Sitting down all day at work, then at the computer in the evening, had been taking a major toll on his health—to say nothing of his diet and drinking: 'The exercise, the walking—that was just instant results. A fifteen-minute walk from work to the station as opposed to taking the shuttle bus; I just felt all the stress and grumpiness about work—it was just gone, I'd forgotten about it. I was just thinking: "What am I going to do tonight?" and looking forward to getting home, as opposed to bringing all that stress home with me, which would sometimes lead to grabbing a drink—and using that to combat the stress.'

For Liz K the difference in well-being she felt at the end of the eight weeks was 'profound', which she put down to being fitter and healthier. She had developed a fear of falling, which made her timid about walking and exercising. Anna-Louise had told her that her fear was justified: 'If you're over the age of 65 you have a 65 per cent chance of falling in a year. If you have had one fall, your chance of having a second fall in twelve months is especially higher.' At the start of the series Liz K was unable to balance on one leg, and her poor sense of balance was compounded by poor sight. 'Fear of falling increases your chance of falling so put all those things together, and you end up with a very high risk of falling,' said Anna-Louise.

But the good news was that by following a simple program of learning to balance on one leg she built up her muscle strength and her confidence. All she had to do was to practise standing on one leg, then the other several times a day, first holding on to something, then learning to do it without that support. Liz K: 'The balance exercise was a treat, and really easy to do. Within the first day I'd gone up to twenty, twenty-five, thirty seconds, and now I can go twenty seconds on each side without holding on.'

The exercises gave her the confidence to build up to 10 000 steps and more each day, which had enormous pay-off for her overall well-being. Liz K: 'The walking has vastly improved my blood pressure, and I think that is the most worthwhile news for anyone, no matter what age you are—keep an eye on your blood pressure and walk or do some form of exercise while you still can. I feel a lot more focused and contented in myself.'

Are you happier?

The undeniable change in all our volunteers was that they all reported feeling happier. Their Happiness 100 scores levels showed that they all raised their happiness levels significantly across eight weeks.

Tony told us: 'I started off thinking, "Hold on, what's this all about? Is this going to help me?" And coming towards the end, it has. I have changed. I'm much happier and more comfortable in myself than I was eight weeks ago.'

Ben was especially eloquent: 'Eight weeks ago I seemed to be letting situations and emotions run my life. I had no direction. I was just floating around and not very happy. Actually really, really unhappy is probably a better way to put it. And now I feel great: I'm happy, I've got direction, and I see the world and experience the world in a different way—in a really full way. It's like all the colours have been reinjected back into the world. It's not black and white any more—it's colourful and bright and vibrant. And I notice it—I don't just let it fly by. I notice things when I talk to people. I notice things when I walk down the street. I interact more with the world now. It feels great to be in control instead of feeling like a runaway train. I feel I am in control of my destiny.'

Now it's your turn

Here are some tips if you want to get the most out of a written, reflective process:

- Write in a way that reveals your deepest thoughts and feelings.[20]
- Write for yourself—not for anyone else.
- Try to be accurate.
- You can write by hand or on a computer.
- Try to express your emotions verbally while writing—it can make a big difference.[21]
- Think about what you are going to write before you start.

- Write freely without worrying about grammar.
- Playing soft music in the background is very helpful.
- To get the most out of this reflective exercise choose a particular time of day to write.
- It's best not to write at bedtime—it can keep you awake.[22]

Apart from helping you to reflect in a constructive, focused fashion—thereby deepening your learning[23]—this kind of writing can also improve both physical and psychological health.[24] Try it.

You have now identified that the steps worked for you. Like the volunteers, some steps will feel like a natural 'fit' for you. Others might feel less natural at first. But rather than dismiss those steps as 'not for me', we suggest that you give them another try. Try them again but maybe do them in a different way. Try the different steps as an 'experiment'. For example, if you found that you keep forgetting to be mindful during your day-to-day activities, you might want to try setting aside ten or fifteen minutes a day at a regular time to sit mindfully. Maybe you could work some formal sit-down mindfulness into your life. What else might work?

The final question to ask yourself is about how you see your future.

How do you see the future?

Rebekah aims to be more open to getting outside her comfort zone: 'Trying new things, looking at the world in a different way. I am going forward with a greater sense of kindness towards myself and the world.'

Liz K is committed to continue the dancing classes that have given her a new lease of life. 'I know that Nick and I will dance for as long as our hips and knees hold out. The thing is I've never felt overwhelmed by old age or by death. But this just makes the adventure still very exciting.'

Cade and Stephen are aware that they need to work on maintaining the momentum, rather than slip back into old patterns of behaviour.

Cade: 'I have got a slight niggling fear that somehow I will slip back in to my old self, but I think I have experienced too much of the good life to let that happen, and I am just too excited about the future to allow myself to shrink back in to the little box that I was in. So I can see a lot of excitement and I see a lot more happiness.'

Stephen: 'It would be too easy to let it slip a bit, but I feel strong and confident that that is not going to happen. I have got a good understanding of the things that were going wrong, and I am not going to lose sight of those things.'

Natalia was clear: 'I see this as the beginning of a journey into the rest of my life, which sounds a bit tacky, but it is really true.'

We hope that is where you are headed, too. We hope that you have found this program as rewarding as the Marrickville Eight. We hope you have enjoyed the journey.

Part 3

Behind the Program

The science

The ground-breaking TV series *Making Australia Happy* took eight volunteers from inner-city Sydney and, with the guidance of an elite happiness coaching team, set out to transform them.

At the beginning of the program we took baseline measurements of physical, neurological, psychological and biological tests, which provided information on our volunteers' brain activity, blood chemistry, diet, sleep patterns and psychological well-being. And we retested them over the course of the program.

A specially selected Happiness Team was drawn from the fields of Positive Psychology, mindfulness and physiotherapy. Together Dr Anthony (Tony) Grant, director of the Coaching Psychology Unit at Sydney University, Dr Russ Harris, GP and a recognised expert in mindfulness, and Anna-Louise Bouvier, expert physiotherapist, supervised their progress.

A shopfront in Marrickville became 'Happiness HQ' for eight weeks as our volunteers and the coaching team set out to prove that anyone, whatever their life situation, can improve their well-being by following a few, scientifically validated Positive Psychology exercises.

The Marrickville Eight

In order to give Positive Psychology a real run for its money we needed diversity, a reasonable cross-section of Australian society. People from different cultural backgrounds. People with a range of occupations. Different ages. Some married. Some single. Some young—some 'not so young'. Some with young children. Some working. Some retired. Real people in real life—with real problems, real dreams and a real desire to be happier.

This program was not designed to treat mental illness, so we had to make sure that the people we selected did not have major mental health or psychiatric problems. Those require specialist treatment from a doctor, psychologist or psychiatrist. We wanted people with a wide range of 'happiness scores'—not just people who were feeling sad or down or depressed. We wanted some 'moderately happy' people, some 'sad' people, and some who were in between. Regular people!

Eventually, after many discussions, including duty-of-care background checks, mental health assessments, consultation with their families and precautionary interviews with a clinical psychologist, we found eight suitable volunteers, the Marrickville Eight.

The Happiness 100 Index Scores

The Marrickville Eight were quite an unhappy bunch when they set out on their journey. Their scores on the Happy 100 Index were pretty low.

As we have already learnt, although happiness is a subjective experience, it can be measured. Thousands of research studies, from individual to whole country populations, use a methodology of this kind to measure happiness scientifically.[1]

We designed the Happy 100 Index so that if you score 50 you are neither happy nor sad overall. Neutral. If you have a score greater

Table 1: Participants' scores in the Happiness 100 Index

Name	Score at Time 1	Score at Time 2	Score at Time 3	Score at Time 4
Cade	30	78	58	85
Liz	46	48	68	75
Stephen	54	64	76	88
Natalia	45	67	66	79
Rebekah	48	76	82	90
Ben	40	49	51	76
Tony	59	85	87	93
Liz K	59	81	86	88

Table 2: Changes in participants' scores in the Happiness 100 Index

Name	Change in score between time 1 and time 2	Change in score between time 2 and time 3	Change in score between time 3 and time 4	Overall change between time 1 and time 4
Cade	+48	−20	+27	+55
Liz	+2	+20	+7	+29
Stephen	+10	+12	+12	+34
Natalia	+22	−1	+13	+34
Rebekah	+28	+6	+8	+42
Ben	+9	+2	+25	+36
Tony	+26	+2	+6	+34
Liz K	+22	+5	+2	+29

than 50, then overall you are more happy than sad. A score of less than 50 meant you are more sad than happy. On the basis of much previous research into well-being and happiness,[2] we would expect the average Australian to score about 70 to 75 on the Happy 100 Index—that was our benchmark. Every single one of the Marrickville Eight scored well below our benchmark on the Happiness 100 Test.

We emphasised again and again to the Marrickville Eight that this was not a competition. They were not competing against each other to see who could be the happiest. This journey was about them as individuals, about their personal happiness potential. If they were competing it was only against themselves.

With Cade scoring 30, Ben scoring 40, Natalia scoring 45, Liz scoring 46, Rebekah scoring 48, Stephen scoring 54 and both Tony and Liz K on 59, all our volunteers had a long way to go to reach the benchmark. This was going to be some journey. Yet eight weeks later there was a dramatic increase in happiness levels across the board. By the end of the series most soared well into the high seventies, eighties and nineties. Liz had the lowest final score out of the whole group (her final score was 75), but even that was 29 points higher than her original score!

As you can see from the tables on page 89, their happiness levels increased step by step as they progressed through the program. From time 1 to time 2, a period of two to three weeks, everyone's score increased.

Cade's Happy 100 journey

From time 1 to time 2 Cade had a dramatic increase of 48 points—he went from a low of 30 up to 78! Part of the reason for the dramatic increase was probably due to the fact that Cade was starting from such a low point. You will recall that Cade had the worst dietary habits in the group and that his activity levels were unbelievably low. When you start off so low, virtually any positive change is going to have a big effect. And it did for Cade. But as is often the case, an initial high increase is often followed by a slip backwards. And this was the case for Cade. His scores between time 2 and time 3 went backwards minus 20 points. His score for time 2 was 78, but his score for time 3 was only 58. What happened?

The experts on the panel agreed that the stresses of actually taking part in the television series, along with trying to make major adaptations to his lifestyle, might have contributed to his lower score. It is important to bear in mind that making purposeful positive change is not easy. Change is difficult. Real change takes effort. Cade put that effort in, and was able to consolidate in the final few weeks ending up with a final score of 85—a huge improvement in just eight weeks.

Liz's Happy 100 journey

Liz had started with a low score of 46 at Time 1. Despite her best efforts in the first few weeks, her score increased by only 2 points to 48. In fact Liz was trying too hard. The big change for Liz came once she started to practise the mindfulness techniques—when she started to do less. Rather than trying to be in control all the time—doing lots of exercise, micromanaging everything down to a T—what worked for Liz was learning to let go. Going with the flow. She made a spectacular increase of 20 points between time 2 and time 3, recording 68 at time 3 and finishing the series at 75—right on our benchmark.

Stephen's Happy 100 journey

Stephen's progression was the steadiest of the whole group. In some ways his progress reflected his character strengths of 'judgement and open-mindedness': thinking things through, being open to ideas and applying oneself in a systematic fashion. Stephen's initial score was the third highest in the group. He was very disappointed by this score as he saw himself as being far happier than that. He saw himself as being a happy person. But the Happy 100 Index measurement told a different story. Although Stephen had quite high levels of positive affect—high levels of positive emotions—he also had very high stress levels. He was severely stressed, and this stress was bringing down his overall score. He really did need to get to grips with the stressors in his life.

Over the next few weeks his stress levels dropped dramatically. His first increase showed a gain of 10 points. His score between time 2 and time 3 increased by 12 points, and his score between time 3 and time 4 increased by 12 points again. Steady, regular improvement. His final score of 88 was well above our benchmark.

Natalia's Happy 100 journey

Natalia was another person who got off to a flying start only to have a setback. Her initial score of 45 at time 1 was boosted by 22 points to 67 at time 2. Between time 1 and time 2 her anxiety and stress reduced significantly; the amount of positive emotions she was experiencing also went up, and she was feeling far less down. However, between time 2 and time 3 her stress levels shot up considerably, partly due to work pressures and having to deal with the demands of filming. Her Happy 100 Index scores at time 3 fell back by minus 1 point to 66.

The forgiveness exercise was a major part of Natalia's journey. Once she had completed this she started to feel far more comfortable with herself. Learning to forgive others seemed to have had an important, if unexpected effect—she was learning to be kinder to herself—and her time 4 score showed that. Her time 4 score increased by 13 points, and she finished with an above-benchmark score of 79.

Rebekah's Happy 100 journey

Rebekah made a spectacular start to her journey. Her score at time 1 was 48—just a tad on the sad side of the 50 'neutral' line. She responded very well to the mindfulness training, and her time 2 scores leapt 28 points to 76. After this massive initial boost in well-being Rebekah continued to make steady progress. It was as if completing the forgiveness exercises and practising mindfulness regularly gave her the tools to consolidate her gains. Her stress and anxiety levels halved between time 1 and time 2. From time 2 to time 3 her score increased another 6 points to 82, and her final time 4 score of 90 was one of the highest. She positively glowed by the end of the series.

Ben's Happy 100 journey

Ben's story is about a rough road. He did not find the initial part of the journey easy. He started with a score at time 1 of 40—the second lowest score after Cade. His score increased by 9 points for a time 2 score of 49—an improvement on his initial score but still under the 50 'neutral' line. Although his overall Happy 100 Index score increased between time 1 and time 2, and the amount of positive emotions he was experiencing increased, he was finding it tough going—his stress and anxiety levels actually went up 27 per cent between time 1 and time 2. Ben found it hard to get to grips with his goals and putting real action into the program. And it showed in his scores. His time 3 score increased by only 2 points—to 51. He was just over the neutral line. However, once Ben realised that he did not have to solve all his problems in one day—and started to just deal with one thing at a time—his scores really shifted. He finished with a final time 4 score of 76, a massive 25 point increase in the final weeks.

Tony's Happy 100 journey

Tony had one of the highest initial scores. His time 1 score was 59—above the neutral line, but still below the benchmark we set. Much of his journey was about rediscovering the values passed on to him by his parents. Once he decided to commit himself to the program, to really work on making change, his scores took off. His time 2 score was up 26 points to 85. In the first few weeks he more than halved his stress levels. And he continued to shine. His time 3 score was 87, a two-point increase, and he finished with the highest score of the group with a time 4 score of 93.

Liz K's Happy 100 journey

Liz K's score closely resembled Tony's. Like Tony, she started with a time 1 score of 59. Her initial increase was similarly large. Her time 2 score went up to 81, an increase of 22 points—great work! Her scores then stabilised somewhat. Her time 3 score was 86, an increase of five points, and well above the benchmark we had set. Delighted with her changes, she consolidated her happiness level, increasing only 2 points to finish with a time 4 score of 88.

Happy mind, happy body

More and more research is showing that happiness is not just about feeling good. If we become emotionally healthier, we also become physically healthier. And conversely, as we become physically healthier, we feel happier, too! It works both ways.

We wanted to put this program to the test. We wanted to see whether the holistic approach to happiness we have designed was truly effective. So we asked all our volunteers to take a battery of physiological tests—before, during and after the program. We wanted rigorous testing.

We checked their mental state. We assessed their anxiety. We measured their emotions. But we also wanted to get physical. We checked their blood, their cholesterol levels, their stress hormones. We looked at their sleeping patterns. We examined their immune responses. These tests are all well-established markers of physical well-being. But we wanted to go further. To new territory.

So, we scanned their brains.

Lifestyle, happiness and our genes

Lifestyle affects the way our genes function. Research is beginning to show that prolonged psychological stress and poor emotional health—such as continuous anxiety, pessimism and deep-seated anger—might increase the risk of genetic mutations.

When people cope badly with stress, the body is less able to repair those mutations. Psychological stress also affects genetic expression; if a person has a predisposition to such illnesses as depression, schizophrenia, addictive behaviour, asthma and autoimmune conditions, continuous stress increases the risk that those genes will be expressed (or turned on). In fact, mental health is now thought to be a major factor in the development, expression and repair of our genes.

Continuous stress might even make us age prematurely. Ageing causes the tips of our genes—the telomeres—to shrink. Telomeres protect our strands of DNA from unravelling by capping them, rather like the little plastic tips on the end of shoelaces. Worn and frayed telomeres lead to chronic disease and death. Continuous and uncontrollable stress appears to accelerate the process. Working with Elizabeth Blackburn, the 2009 winner of the Nobel Prize for Medicine and Physiology on her pioneering work on the function of telomeres, Elissa Epel at the University of California has spent the last decade studying pre-menopausal women who have been caring for handicapped children or loved ones with dementia. The women who were not coping with the stress were nine to seventeen years older genetically than the same age-group who were able to cope.[*]

However, in an exciting new development, the team has shown that vigorous exercise can offset the impact of the stress.[†] Among the highly stressed women they are monitoring, only the inactive ones had shorter telomeres. Those who were exercising regularly had not suffered similar damage.

The team has also shown that chronic pessimism has the same effect on our genetic age: it too shortens telomeres.[‡] Future research might even show that optimism will preserve or even lengthen our telomeres and help us to live longer, which is somewhat speculative but fascinating. We shall see. The story about genetics and happiness has yet to be fully told.

[*] Epel, E.S., Blackburn, E.H., Lin, J. et al., 'Accelerated telomere shortening in response to life stress', *Proceedings of the National Academy of Sciences of the United States of America*, vol. 101, 2004, pp. 17312–15.

[†] Puterman, E., Lin, J., Blackburn, E. et al., 'The power of exercise: Buffering the effect of chronic stress on telomere length', www.plosone.org/article/info:doi/10.1371/journal.pone.0010837 (retrieved 17 June 2010).

[‡] O'Donovan, A., Lin, J., Dhabhar, F.S. et al., 'Pessimism correlates with leukocyte telomere shortness and elevated interleukin-6 in post-menopausal women', *Brain, Behavior, and Immunity*, vol. 23, 2009, pp. 446–9.

As Dr Craig Hassed, GP and senior lecturer at Monash University Department of General Practice, and consultant to *Making Australia Happy*, says, 'A healthy and happy mind is fundamental for a healthy body.' In his book *The Essence of Health* he describes the intimate mind–body connection that is essential for mental and physical health. 'The mechanisms are infinitely complex, but the principle is infinitely simple,' he writes.[3]

Although our program is unique—no one has done something quite like this before—the existing scientific research literature suggested that we would see measurable physiological improvements in all these areas. And we did. Across the board we saw that as the Marrickville Eight's happiness levels increased there were also tangible and substantial physiological changes. And this was in just eight weeks.

The hard data collected from biological and physiological measures such as blood pressure, cholesterol, hormones and brain functioning gives further validation that this kind of positive psychology program can be truly effective. It works!

The essentials: exercise and sleep

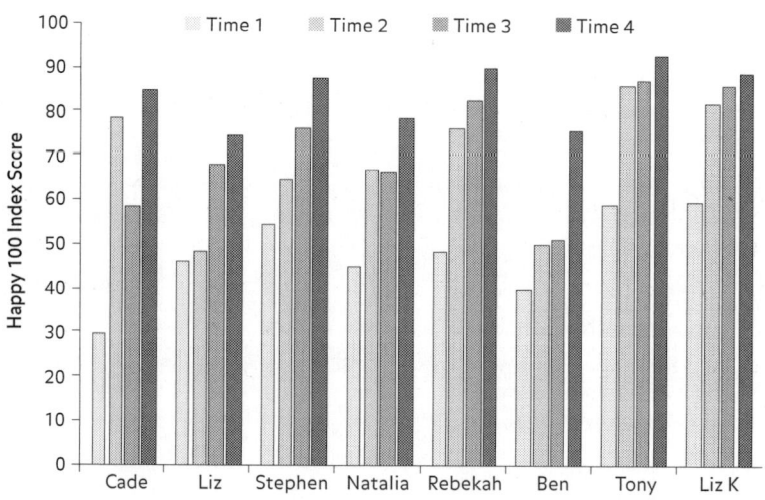

Figure 1: Participants' scores in the Happiness 100 Index at different times

We began by finding out whether our volunteers did any exercise (if at all) and whether they slept well (or not). Both are essential ingredients for overall well-being.

We needed to find a way of collecting hard objective data about their physical state. Facts. Not opinions. We needed a way to monitor them twenty-four hours a day, seven days a week.

We asked them all to wear a small lightweight armband, about the size of a large watch, for the full eight-week duration of the program. This little gadget, called SenseWear®, is so sophisticated it can record exactly how much or how little a person moves, even in their sleep, and the intensity of that movement.[4] You can't get away with much. It can even detect when you are having sex!

The computer printouts from the armband revealed that most of our volunteers, apart from Liz and Rebekah who did lots and lots of exercise, were highly sedentary, sleeping poorly and not getting to bed early enough.

Cade, Natalia and Tony had particularly shocking sleep patterns at the start. By the end of the program their armband data showed huge improvements in their sleep patterns and levels of exercise—from virtually no exercise at all they ended up in the 'moderate to vigorous' exercise category—and walking in the region of the recommended 10 000 steps each day!

Biochemical markers

In addition to hard data about sleep and physical movement, we were also interested in biochemical markers of well-being. A biochemical marker is a hormone, antibody, enzyme or other measurable biological substance that is detected in the body and acts as a sign of either a disease or some abnormality or positive aspects of health such as well-being.

Cortisol

First we looked at cortisol, the hormone you pump out when you're wrestling with metaphorical tigers. People living stressful lives are often in a semi-permanent state of stress response, which affects our physical and mental health. Cortisol influences many aspects of health, including immunity, our risk of developing metabolic syndrome (see below), the storage of fat and the health of our bones.

By measuring cortisol levels in our volunteers' saliva on three separate days once in week 1, once in week 4 and once in week 8, we aimed to get a picture of their stress levels before, during and after the Eight Steps program.

Cortisol levels are normally higher in the mornings and lower at night, so to allow for these variations we took five samples from each person over the course of those days, and we also took account of any particularly stressful circumstances that could have influenced the readings.

We were not surprised to find that at the start of the series most of the participants—six out of eight—had unhealthy levels. It was notable that the cortisol levels actually increased even further during the first three or four weeks. That was to be expected to begin with, as making so many changes and taking on so many challenges is stressful in itself.

Change can be stressful. As you start the Eight Steps program you might find that your stress initially increases. Not everyone will have this experience, though. But if you do feel a bit stressed or overwhelmed, persevere. The first few weeks could be a potentially tricky patch as you begin to step out of your comfort zone. But this is a very important time. Once you get through this period, as we saw with our participants, things will start to come back into balance.

At the end of the eight weeks their overall cortisol levels and stress patterns had dropped dramatically, and virtually everybody attained a normal healthy pattern.

So, be flexible. Some people might find it a bit much to fit these steps into eight weeks—although it can be done quite easily. But if you want to take longer, then do so. Although we know the eight-week time frame works—and works well—your own personal Eight Steps program need not be constrained by a schedule of just eight weeks if you feel it is too much. Take a bit longer. Be flexible. After all, this is for your enjoyment, your happiness, your life.

Melatonin

The hormone melatonin is secreted by the pineal gland in the brain and is a very useful biochemical marker for a range of reasons. It not only regulates our sleep but also helps to regulate other hormones. It is an indicator of our capacity to deal with stress,[5] is thought to influence immunity and genetic function and might have cancer protective effects.[6] Reducing stress and taking steps to enjoy a healthy lifestyle boosts melatonin.[7]

This is very important when it comes to getting a good night's sleep, which is an essential component of good physical and mental health. Melatonin is the hormone that regulates our sleep/wake cycle. It plays a critical role in when we fall asleep and when we wake up. We checked the volunteers' melatonin levels at midnight. Five of our participants had low levels of melatonin to begin with, but by the end of the experiment there was an average 60 per cent increase in melatonin levels across the group, another indication that their healthy lifestyle changes were making a difference.

Metabolic markers

Metabolic syndrome

Metabolic syndrome is common in developed countries living the so-called Western lifestyle of inactivity, high stress and poor diet.

Metabolic syndrome is a cluster of risk factors that include high blood pressure, high cholesterol, high blood glucose (type 2 diabetes) and central obesity. High cortisol levels promote weight gain around the trunk. It has major implications for the development of other problems like heart disease. We therefore wanted to measure some markers of metabolic syndrome and see how they responded to stress reduction and lifestyle change.

High stress levels are one of the main drivers of metabolic syndrome because they create prolonged wear and tear on the body, known as allostatic load.

Blood pressure

Blood pressure is the measure of the pressure of blood in your arteries as it is pumped by your heart. High blood pressure usually indicates that the body is stressed.

When we are stressed our heart is working overtime, putting pressure on other organs. High blood pressure can lead to serious problems, such as a heart attack, a stroke, heart failure or kidney disease. But here's the good news: blood pressure is very responsive to positive lifestyle changes and stress reduction.[8]

Five of the eight volunteers had normal blood pressure at the start of filming, and remained in the normal range at the end. But there were three whose blood pressure caused concern. After eight weeks, with the range of Positive Psychology interventions, increased exercise and focus on well-being, the group of three experienced a significant reduction in blood pressure (in technical terms this was an average drop of 35/16). Dr Hassed says, 'You would expect to see a drop of 15 over 10 in response to lifestyle changes. This was a very major drop and comparable to what you would expect if you took medication to reduce your blood pressure.'

Cholesterol levels

High cholesterol levels, like high blood pressure, is one of a number of factors that increases the risk of developing cardiovascular disease. As with high blood pressure, the higher your blood cholesterol level, the greater your risk of developing heart disease or having a heart attack. But cholesterol levels respond to lifestyle changes and stress reduction.

At the start of filming, half the group had high cholesterol levels. By the end of the series, all were within normal range, with one exception, which was now only minimally high. The overall reduction for most participants was 0.5 of a point, and in one case 0.8. This is a significant change, particularly without medication.

The volunteers are living proof that when people make and maintain healthy lifestyle changes, such as adopting a positive outlook, improving their diet and exercising more, the problems of metabolic syndrome start to recede.

Immunity

The immune system is the body's main line of defence against disease and infections.

New research in the emerging field of psychoneuroimmunology suggests that people who have positive emotions and cope well with stress can enhance their immunity whereas people who perceive the world in a negative way and respond poorly to events have a suppressed immunity system that makes them more susceptible to disease.[9] A number of experiments have been able to demonstrate this by measuring the level of immunoglobulin antibodies in saliva (S-IgA) in a range of scenarios. S-IgA is our front-line defence against viruses that trigger coughs and colds and gastrointestinal infections.

One study looked at how the immune system responded to anger compared to compassion.[10] After inducing the positive emotions of compassion in a group of people for just five minutes their immune levels shot up. When the study repeated the process, only this time inducing anger, immune levels went down significantly. The effects lasted for up to five hours. Anger does take its toll. And the effects might last longer than we think.

Depending on one's emotional response, even watching a film can boost immunity. In a classic Harvard University experiment a group of students were shown a film of Mother Teresa helping the sick and the dying in the slums of Calcutta.[11] Saliva tests showed an increase in antibody levels after the screening. But what was really surprising was that, despite some of the group feeling cynical about Mother Teresa, watching altruistic behaviour still had a positive physiological effect on them.

With this in mind we randomly selected four of our eight volunteers to explore the influence of altruistic behaviour on them. We tested their saliva on a day when they had been helping out at the Exodus Foundation, a charity that works with some of the most needy people in society. The charity runs a free restaurant for anybody who's hungry and regularly feeds around 400 people every day.

We tested our volunteers before they started helping out, and again at the end of the day's altruistic activities. As we expected, their immunoglobulin levels all increased—an average of 36 per cent—which would indicate that they would have had significantly higher resistance to infection afterwards.

If engaging in altruistic activities benefits your physical health after just a few hours, imagine the benefits if you live your whole life altruistically.

Does positivity increase pain tolerance?

Empirical research has been accumulating support for the theory that positive emotions give us an evolutionary advantage—that they build our intellectual, social and physical resources. This theory, originally proposed by psychologist Barbara Fredrickson, holds that we're much more likely to think clearly and creatively when we are in a positive frame of mind as opposed to stressed or depressed.[12] With a positive outlook we are more likely to develop friendships and relationships that sustain us, and we are more likely to be healthier and live longer. All of which gives us the edge when it comes to survival.

One common finding from studies is that positive emotions help to build resilience, an essential trait for survival.[13] One way to demonstrate that is to see whether high levels of optimism and hope correlate with high pain tolerance. If our Eight Steps program was indeed effective then, according to the theory, our volunteers should be able to tolerate more pain once they had finished the program! To this end we made our volunteers dunk their hand and wrist in ice cold water—the cold presser test—to see how long they could tolerate the pain at the beginning and at the end of the Eight Steps program. If the Positive Psychology coaching over eight weeks had done its job, their average pain tolerance should have increased and they would be able to keep their wrists submerged for longer.

We based this on a famous experiment that put two groups of people through the cold presser test. One group received fifteen minutes prior coaching where they were told to focus on mental images of hope and positive thoughts, such as successful accomplishment of goals, while the other group received no coaching. In that study the group with the positive coaching lasted twice as long in the iced water as the control group.[14]

Amazingly, we saw similar results with our volunteers. At the beginning of the series, the average amount of time they could tolerate the pain was 57 seconds. After the eight-week program the average time had increased to 131 seconds, well over double the original score!

While the *Making Australia Happy* experiment was not conducted under rigorous scientific conditions—for example, we did not use a control group—our program consultants confirm that the results indicate how positive emotions can build our physical strength and our emotional resilience.

Brain scans

Excited by all these findings, we wondered whether the behavioural changes that our volunteers had made by following the Happiness program would also be reflected in neurological changes in their brains.

Richard J. Davidson at the University of Wisconsin was one of the first to use brain imaging to study the neurological influence of mind over matter. In his seminal study published in 2004, he compared what was happening in the brains of Buddhists monks with inexperienced volunteers when they were asked to perform 'compassion meditation', concentrating on directing loving and compassionate thoughts towards others. The research showed that the level of activity in the areas of the brain associated with regulating emotions was much higher in the brains of the Buddhist monks than in the novices. What's more, the altered brain pattern appeared to last for some time after the formal periods of meditation.[15] It was the first hard-nosed evidence that meditation was actually redirecting the neural networks and might even be inducing long-term neural changes.

Since then Davidson and others have produced a stream of studies that demonstrate variations on this phenomenon. They have shown that experienced meditators can focus the brain away from unwanted or disturbing emotions. Compared to novices, experienced meditators show more activity in the areas of the brain that deal with paying attention and keeping focus and less activity in the areas that respond to thoughts and emotions, and they can maintain that focus even when the scientists try to distract them.

For the *Making Australia Happy* television series we turned to Associate Professor Mark Williams at Macquarie University's Centre for Cognitive Science. His research focuses on the cognitive and neural mechanisms involved in face and facial expression perception and in processing objects and complex scenes. He uses neuroimaging techniques such as functional magnetic resonance (fMRI) and magnetoencephalography (MEG) scans to pinpoint where and when these processes happen in the brain. MEG is state of the art brain imaging. The MEG scanner at Macquarie is the only one of its kind in the Southern Hemisphere.

Dr Williams scanned the brains of our volunteers in the week before the start of the happiness regime and again at the end of the series eight weeks later. The MEG scanner monitored the activity in their parietal and temporal lobes while the volunteers were shown a series of faces expressing happy, sad and neutral emotions. The temporal lobe is associated with perceiving, analysing and recognising objects and faces, while the parietal lobe is involved with paying attention.

On the basis of prior research, Williams expected that after undergoing the full eight-week happiness program we would find a change in the levels of brain activity in our volunteers. And that is exactly what happened.

A quiet brain is a happy brain

At the end of the eight weeks there was a significant decrease in neural activity: around 50 per cent on average, and far greater than he was expecting. 'It's really exciting to see that we could get such a big change,' says Williams. 'It's showing us that at some level plasticity, or an ability to adapt to experience, is occurring.'

Although a decrease in activity might sound counterintuitive, Williams says it correlates with other studies that seem to indicate that a stressed brain is an overactive brain and a happier brain is a more peaceful one. He thinks there are two likely explanations for the results. One is that our volunteers became happier and more relaxed as the program went on. He points to a recent study that demonstrated a similar decrease in neural activity in these same limbic areas when subjects were relaxed from listening to pleasing music.[16]

The other possible explanation for our brain scan results is that our volunteers have actually become better at focusing their attention and maintaining that focus. They don't need to work as hard.

'You can compare our findings to another study[17] which used the stimulus of pain rather than faces to compare two conditions,' says Williams. 'They showed that people trained in meditation have 40 to 50 per cent less activity in the limbic system than the control group when both groups are subjected to pain. They feel the same amount of pain, but their attention is focused elsewhere.'

'The findings are consistent with what we'd expect from mindfulness training,' says Dr Russ Harris, our resident mindfulness expert. 'Mindfulness teaches us to be focused and to engage in the present moment instead of getting caught up in mind chatter. It's a crucial component of the Happiness program, and we know that, as people become more mindful, more engaged, they often become more relaxed.'

'A quiet brain is a happy brain and an efficient brain,' says Dr Craig Hassed, the program's consultant physician. 'What we're doing most of the time is thinking so much, worrying so much, projecting so much that we create a lot of noise in our mind, and you can measure that in brain activity.'

Final thoughts

Modern science is telling us what the ancients have known for thousands of years: that it's an artificial distinction to talk about mind and body as if they were separate. They are intimately connected. When mind and body are working together in sync the body has an incredible capacity to heal and to move us towards being truly happy.

While the number of participants in *Making Australia Happy* was small, the results are clearly remarkable. What's more, our results reflect the findings from thousands of international studies.

Were our results entirely due to the Eight Steps program, or were there other causal factors at play? This was a real-life study. It was not done in the confines of a laboratory, but in people's lives. On the streets. In their homes. And it was filmed.

It is entirely possible that being under the constant scrutiny of the TV cameras, or simply being the centre of attention as part of an original real-life experiment, could have influenced the results. And it is to be expected that these factors would have had some influence on the outcome. But these factors were not always helpful in terms of inducing happiness. Being the centre of attention, being filmed, being watched, having to stick to a timetable, putting time and effort into being a part of a TV program can be stressful and frustrating. The demands of filming are indeed challenging.

The fact that our volunteers did this as part of a TV program must be taken into account when considering these results. Nevertheless, the results are impressive—even outstanding. The Marrickville Eight did change. It worked for them. And it can work for you.

Onwards!

As you will have found out, it's not hard to *become* happy. But it is hard to *stay happy* all the time. In fact it's impossible. Life changes.

Things do get you down. Life is difficult. Shit happens. But, as the Marrickville Eight have shown, we don't have to be trapped by the downtimes. We can bounce back. We can recover. And we can learn to recover quite quickly. Yes—we can!

The key point is to continue to work through these steps. Remember—happiness is a by-product of a well-lived life. Do it! Turn your insights into actions and your actions into habits. The happiness mindset is a habit. Make it habitual.

So, here we are. The end? Well, this might be the end of the book— but it's certainly not the end of the journey. See you on the road. Onwards!

The experts

Dr Tony Grant

Coaching psychologist

Heading our team of experts is Dr Anthony (Tony) Grant. He is an academic, practitioner and international pioneer in the fields of coaching psychology and Positive Psychology. Coaching psychology is about helping people lead more productive, rewarding and happier lives. In 2000 Tony founded the world's first Coaching Psychology Unit at the University of Sydney. In 2009 he was awarded the Vision of Excellence Award from Harvard University for his pioneering work in helping to develop a scientific foundation to coaching. As an author and researcher, Tony has written six books and more than sixty journal articles and book chapters. He has twice received the Excellence in Teaching Award from the University of Sydney (2002 and 2008). Whether teaching his students, coaching business executives or speaking at conferences, Tony combines solid scientific theory with extensive practical experience and a unique sense of humour. In *Making Australia Happy*, he draws on the best evidence-based techniques from coaching and positive psychology to take the message to the streets.

Dr Russ Harris

Mindfulness coach

As the title of his international bestseller *The Happiness Trap* suggests, Dr Russ Harris brings a very different perspective to the subject of happiness. Coming from a mindfulness-based approach, which acknowledges that negative thoughts and emotions are an inevitable part of the human condition, Russ is Australia's foremost specialist in Acceptance and Commitment Therapy (ACT). ACT differs from other mindfulness-based models in that it teaches mindfulness skills through quick, simple exercises rather than the more traditional method of meditation. Through his books, workshops and clinical practice, Russ has helped thousands of people around the world find a richer, more meaningful life. Based in Perth, Russ is a qualified medical practitioner, therapist and life coach.

Anna-Louise Bouvier

Physiotherapist and mind-body specialist

With the volunteers' minds in good hands, leading physiotherapist Anna-Louise Bouvier was recruited to look after their bodies. Based in Sydney, Anna-Louise works in her clinical practice with both elite athletes (she is consultant to the NSW Waratahs Rugby Union team) and the general public. Her Physiocise program helps thousands of people every week who suffer from neck and back pain. As a well-known media commentator, author and journalist, Anna-Louise provides expertise in the area of health and well-being. Previously named Australian Fitness Presenter of the Year, she appears regularly on the *Today Show* and ABC Radio and writes for *Life etc* among other magazines. In 2010 she released her latest book, *The Feel Good Body*, which combines cutting-edge research with practical advice for optimising physical health.

The producers

Jennifer Cummins

Producer

'The Making Australia Happy volunteers were just so open and brave—it takes a lot of courage to lay yourself bare on national television, and I think our viewers will find their journeys incredibly inspiring. Using a series of science-backed strategies, they have faced their demons and really changed their lives. And it's those moments of real revelation, real change, on screen that make me think, "That's why we make documentaries."'

Jennifer Cummins is the principal of Heiress Films, the multi-award-winning factual and documentary company behind the *Making Australia Happy* series. Taking three years from concept to delivery, *Making Australia Happy* has been a labour of love for Jennifer, and reflects her commitment to exploring contemporary issues sensitively via factual television for big audiences.

In addition to *Making Australia Happy* she is also producer of the acclaimed *Life* series, a long-running observational series that tracks a group of children from their first year of life. *Life at 5* airs on ABC television in 2010. Her credits include the Logie-nominated documentary, *From Korea with Love*, the SBS TV series *Hotspell*, and *I, Psychopath*. Before establishing Heiress Films, Jennifer was Manager, Factual Development at the ABC, where she fostered a broad range of new projects covering factual entertainment, arts, history and documentary.

Daryl Karp

Executive producer

'The series works because it applies the science of happiness to real people, facing real issues in their everyday lives. We didn't compromise on the science, and we didn't know whether our experiment to improve the happiness of eight people over eight weeks would genuinely work. So it was a really rewarding experience to see the transformations that took place and to realise that most people could apply these simple, scientifically validated techniques to improve their own well-being.'

Daryl Karp is a senior television executive with extensive experience in science, documentary and factual program-making. Her documentaries have garnered numerous awards, including two gold awards at the New York Film Festival. In addition to *Making Australia Happy*, she is currently executive producer of the multi-award-winning *Life* series for the ABC and *Lost Soldiers of Fromelles* for Channel 7.

She was CEO of Film Australia from 2004 to 2008, and before that held various positions at ABC Television, including Head of Factual Programs and Head of Features and Documentaries, where she was responsible for numerous successful prime-time series.

She has worked with many of the world's major public and factual broadcasters, including the BBC, Channel 4, Channel 5, the Discovery Channel, National Geographic Channel and PBS.

Will Parry

Series producer

'What appealed to me about *Making Australia Happy* was the notion that there are scientifically proven routes to happiness. I loved the idea of taking the science out of the laboratory, and seeing what happens to real people when they had the guidance of our experts to apply it to their daily lives.'

Will was the series producer on the Lifestyle Channel series *Lush House* in 2009. Before that, he lived in New York for six years where he worked primarily for BBC Production USA, and directed the pilot (and multiple subsequent episodes) of the US version of *What Not to Wear* for TLC. He was also the pilot director for the US version of *Come Dine with Me*. In 2006 he was the American location director on *Poem for 9/11*, which won the British Royal Television Society Award for best arts documentary. Until 2002 he ran his own production company in the UK and worked as a producer and director on a variety of documentary and factual entertainment projects for the BBC, Channel 4 and Channel 5.

Kalita Corrigan

Director

'*Making Australia Happy* is a hybrid series, so the biggest challenge for me was to successfully combine the elements of observational documentary, science and entertainment while remaining sensitive to the characters' journeys, and without diluting the science.'

Kalita is a director and producer with more than thirteen years experience in documentary and factual entertainment for broadcast television. Originally from the NSW North Coast, Kalita worked for the BBC and Channel 4 in London for nine years before returning to Australia three years ago. She has extensive experience in producing and directing formatted documentary series as well as long-form observational and science documentaries. Her recent credits include *Roadtrip Nation* for SBS and PBS, series 2 of *The Biggest Loser* for Channel 10, and *Science of Sex* for Channel 5 (UK). *Wanted Down Under*, which she produced and directed for the BBC, was nominated for a Royal Television Society Award for best factual program.

Danielle Brigham

Associate producer, researcher and website producer

'I was amazed by the wealth of fascinating research that exists on the "science of happiness", and, unlike other subjects, which generally have a beginning and end point, there are no limits to what constitutes (or obstructs) human happiness. It was certainly a challenge to refine these complex, sometimes abstract concepts into a three-hour "how to" guide to happiness, but I think the core concepts have all come through in the series.'

Researching the science of happiness might sound like a made-up job, but for Danielle Brigham, it was a reality that stretched over two years. As associate producer, she played a key role in the development and production of the series. She also wrote and produced the accompanying website for ABC online. Her recent research credits include the feature-length documentaries *Mother of Rock: Lillian Roxon* (2010) and *I, Psychopath* (2009). She also worked on *Life at 5* (ABC, 2010), *ADbc* (SBS, 2009) and *Eurovision* (SBS, 2009). Before that, Danielle freelanced for some of the UK's top independent production companies and the BBC in London. With a background in journalism, Danielle also worked for two years in Dublin, as staff writer and website editor for *Hot Press* magazine.

Notes

Introduction

1 Cummins, R., Hamilton, L., Lai, L. et al., 'The well-being of Australians— Differences between statistical sub-divisions, towns and cities', Australian Unity Well-being Index: Report 191 2008, www.deakin.edu.au/research/ acqol/auwbi/survey-reports/survey-2019-2011-report-part-a.pdf (retrieved 14 May 2010).

Becoming happy

1 Vella-Brodrick, D., Park, N. & Peterson, C., 'Three ways to be happy: Pleasure, engagement, and meaning—findings from Australian and US samples', *Social Indicators Research*, vol. 90, 2009, pp. 165–79.

2 Ibid.

3 King, L.A., Hicks, J.A., Krull, J.L. et al., 'Positive affect and the experience of meaning in life', *Journal of Personality and Social Psychology*, vol. 90, 2006, pp. 179–96.

4 Lyubomirsky, S., Sheldon, K. & Schkade, D., 'Pursuing happiness: The architecture of sustainable change', *Review of General Psychology*, vol. 9, 2005, pp. 111–31.

5 Sin, N. & Lyubomirsky, S., 'Enhancing well-being and alleviating depressive symptoms with positive psychology interventions: A practice-friendly meta-analysis', *Journal of Clinical Psychology: In Session*, vol. 65, 2009, pp. 467–87.

6 Diener, E., 'Myths in the science of happiness and directions for future research', in Eid, M. & Larsen R.J. (eds), *The Science of Subjective Well-Being*, Guilford Press, New York, 2008, pp. 493–514.

7 Coca-Cola, 'Open Happiness', www.thecoca-colacompany.com/ openhappiness/2009 (retrieved 3 May 2010).

8 Bankwest, 'Happy Banking: An initiative from Bankwest', www.bankwest. com.au (retrieved 2 May 2010).

9 Ehrenreich, B., *Bright-sided: How the Relentless Promotion of Positive Thinking has Undermined America*, Metropolitan Books, New York, 2009.

10 Held, B.S., 'The tyranny of the positive attitude in America: Observation and speculation', *Journal of Clinical Psychology*, vol. 58, 2002, pp. 965–92.

11 Nemeth, C.J., Personnaz, M., Personnaz, B. et al., 'The liberating role of conflict in group creativity: A cross-cultural study', UC Berkeley, Institute for Research on Labor and Employment 2003, http://escholarship.org/uc/item/2014k2070n2017v2018 (retrieved 2 May 2010).

12 Prochaska, J.O. & DiClemente, C.C., 'Toward a comprehensive model of change', in Prochaska, J.O. & DiClemente, C.C. (eds), *The Transtheoretical Approach: Crossing the Traditional Boundaries of Therapy*, Dow-Jones, Homewood, IL, 1984.

Challenging assumptions

1 Seligman, M.E. & Csikszentmihalyi, M., 'Positive psychology: An introduction', *American Psychologist*, vol. 55, 2000, pp. 5–14.

2 Zhong, J.Y. & Mitchell, V.-W., 'A mechanism model of the effect of hedonic product consumption on well-being', *Journal of Consumer Psychology*, vol. 20, 2010, pp. 152–62.

3 Diener, E. & Biswas-Diener, R., 'Will money increase subjective well-being? A literature review and guide to needed research', in Diener, E. (ed.), *The Science of Well-being: The Collected Works of Ed Diener*, Springer, New York, 2009, pp. 119–54.

4 Eaton, W.W., Anthony, J.C., Mandel, W. et al., 'Occupations and the prevalence of major depressive disorder, *Journal of Occupational and Environmental Medicine*, vol. 32, 1990, pp. 1079–87.

5 Diener & Biswas-Diener, 'Will money increase subjective well-being?'.

6 Cameron, K.S., Dutton, J.E. & Quinn, R.E. (eds), *Positive Organizational Scholarship: Foundations of a New Discipline*, Berrett-Koehler, San Francisco, 2003.

7 Wallis, C., 'The new science of happiness', *Time*, 2005, www.time.com/time/magazine/article/2010,9171,1015902,1015900.html (retrieved 5 May 2010).

8 Fowler, J.H. & Christakis, N.A., 'Dynamic spread of happiness in a large social network: Longitudinal analysis over 20 years in the Framingham Heart Study', *British Medical Journal*, vol. 338, 2008, pp. 24–7.

9 Frisch, M.B., *Quality of Life Therapy: Applying a Life Satisfaction Approach to Positive Psychology and Cognitive Therapy*, John Wiley & Sons, New York, 2006, pp. xiii, 353.

10 Senay, I., Albarracin, D. & Noguchi, K., 'Motivating goal-directed behavior through introspective self-talk', *Psychological Science*, vol. 21, 2010, pp. 499–504.

11 Wood, J.V., Perunovic, W.Q.E. & Lee, J.W., 'Positive Self-statements: Power for some, peril for others', *Psychological Science*, vol. 20, 2009, pp. 860–6.

12 MacLeod, C., Mathews, A. & Tata, P., 'Attentional bias in emotional disorders', *Journal of Abnormal Psychology*, vol. 95, 1986, pp. 15–20.

13 Constans, J.I., Penn, D.L., Ihen, G.H. et al., 'Interpretive biases for ambiguous stimuli in social anxiety', *Behaviour Research and Therapy*, vol. 37, 1999, pp. 643–51.

14 Mogg, K., Bradley, B., Williams, R. et al., 'Subliminal processing of emotional information in anxiety and depression', *Journal of Abnormal Psychology*, vol. 102, 1993, pp. 304–11.

15 Kabat-Zinn, J., 'Mindfulness-based interventions in context: Past, present, and future', *Clinical Psychology: Science and Practice*, vol. 10, 2003, pp. 144–56.

16 Paul, G., Ludger, N., Stefan, S. et al., 'Mindfulness-based stress reduction and health benefits: A meta-analysis', *Journal of Psychosomatic Research*, vol. 57, 2004, pp. 35–43.

17 Davidson, R.J. & Lutz, A., 'Buddha's brain: Neuroplasticity and meditation', *IEEE Signal Processing Magazine*, 2008, http://psyphz.psych.wisc.edu/web/pubs/2008/buddha_brain_IEEE.pdf (retrieved 7 May 2010).

18 Harbaugh, W.T., Mayr, U. & Burghart, D.R., 'Neural responses to taxation and voluntary giving reveal motives for charitable donations', *Science*, vol. 316, 2007, pp. 1622–5.

19 Lutz, A., Greischar, L.L., Rawlings, N.B. et al., 'Long-term meditators self-induce high-amplitude gamma synchrony during mental practice', *Proceedings of the National Academy of Sciences of the United States of America*, vol. 101, 2004, pp. 16369–73.

20 Didonna, F. (ed.), *Clinical Handbook of Mindfulness*, Springer-Verlag, New York, 2008.

21 Amishi, P., Jha, J.K. & Baim, M., 'Mindfulness training modifies subsystems of attention', *Cognitive, Affective and Behavioral Neuroscience*, vol. 7, 2007, pp. 109–19.

22 Zeidan, F., Johnson, S.K., Diamond, B.J. et al., 'Mindfulness meditation improves cognition: Evidence of brief mental training', *Consciousness and Cognition*, vol. 19, 2010, pp. 597–605.

Making changes

1   Izard, C.E., 'Basic emotions, relations among emotions, and emotion-cognition relations', *Psychological Review*, vol. 99, 1992, pp. 561–5.

2   Petty, R.E., Tormala, Z.L., Briñol, P. et al., 'Implicit ambivalence from attitude change: An exploration of the PAST model', *Journal of Personality and Social Psychology*, vol. 90, 2006, pp. 21–41.

3   Grant, A.M. & Greene, J., *Coach Yourself: Make Real Change in Your Life*, 2nd edn, Momentum Press, London, 2004.

4   Latham, G.P. & Locke, E.A., 'New developments in and directions for goal-setting research', *European Psychologist*, vol. 12, 2007, pp. 290–300.

5   Hart, R.R., 'Therapeutic effectiveness of setting and monitoring goals', *Journal of Consulting and Clinical Psychology*, vol. 46, 1978, pp. 1242–5.

6   Fava, G.A. & Ruini, C., 'Development and characteristics of a well-being enhancing psychotherapeutic strategy: Well-being therapy', *Journal of Behavior Therapy and Experimental Psychiatry*, vol. 34, 2003, pp. 45–63.

7   Harris, C., Daniels, K. & Briner, R.B., 'A daily diary study of goals and affective well-being at work', *Journal of Occupational and Organizational Psychology*, vol. 76, 2003, pp. 401–10.

8   Sheldon, K.M., Ryan, R. & Reis, H.T., 'What makes for a good day? Competence and autonomy in the day and in the person', *Personality and Social Psychology Bulletin*, vol. 22, 1996, pp. 1270–9.

9   Science Daily, 'Upright walking began 6 million years ago', 2008, www.sciencedaily.com/releases/2008/03/080320183657.htm (retrieved 17 May 2010).

10 Dunstan, D.W., 'Television viewing time and mortality: The Australian Diabetes, Obesity and Lifestyle Study (AusDiab)', *Journal of the American Heart Association*, 12 January 2010.

11 Thorp, A. & Dunstan, D., *Stand Up, Australia: Sedentary Behaviour in Workers*, Baker IDI Heart and Diabetes Institute, University of Queensland, and Medibank Private, 2009.

12 Central Queensland University, Rockhampton, and Queensland Health, 'The 10 000 steps challenge', www.10000steps.org.au (retrieved 17 May 2010).

13 Lavelle, P., '10 000 steps and counting', ABC Health and Well-being, 2007, www.abc.net.au/health/thepulse/stories/2007/11/29/2104899.htm (retrieved 17 May 2010).

14 10 000 Steps. Visit www.10000steps.org.au for more ideas on how to get moving.

15 Murray, C. & Lopez, A., *The Global Burden of Disease: A Comprehensive Assessment of Mortality and Disability from Diseases, Injuries, and Risk*

Factors in 1990 and Projected to 2020, Harvard University Press, Cambridge, MA, 1990.

16 Jacka, F.N., Pasco, J.A., Mykletun A. et al., 'Association of Western and traditional diets with depression and anxiety in women', *American Journal of Psychiatry*, 2010, vol. 167, no. 3, pp. 305–11.

17 Sanchez-Villegas, A., Delgado-Rodriguez, M., Alonso, A. et al., 'Association of the Mediterranean dietary pattern with the incidence of depression: The Seguimiento Universidad de Navarra/University of Navarra follow-up (SUN) cohort', *Archives of General Psychiatry*, vol. 66, 2009, pp. 1090–8.

18 Akbaraly, T.N., Brunner, E.J., Ferrie, J.E. et al., 'Dietary pattern and depressive symptoms in middle age', *British Journal of Psychiatry*, vol. 195, 2009, pp. 408–13.

19 Greenwood, C.E. & Winocur, G., 'Learning and memory impairment in rats fed a high saturated fat diet', *Behavioral and Neural Biology*, vol. 53, 1990, pp. 74–87.

20 Johnson, P.M. & Kenny, P.J., 'Dopamine D2 receptors in addiction-like reward dysfunction and compulsive eating in obese rats', *Nature Neuroscience*, vol. 13, 2010, pp. 635–41.

21 Parker, G., Gibson, N.A., Brotchie, H. et al., 'Omega-3 fatty acids and mood disorders', *American Journal of Psychiatry*, vol. 163, 2006, pp. 969–78.

22 Avena, N.M., Rada, P. & Hoebel, B.G., 'Evidence for sugar addiction: Behavioral and neurochemical effects of intermittent, excessive sugar intake', *Neuroscience and Biobehavioral Reviews*, vol. 32, 2008, pp. 20–39.

23 For the Australian Dietary Guidelines for Adults, see www.nhmrc.gov.au/_files_nhmrc/file/publications/synopses/n33.pdf.

24 Rosen, I.M., Gimotty, P.A., Shea, J.A. et al., 'Evolution of sleep quantity, sleep deprivation, mood disturbances, empathy, and burnout among interns', *Academic Medicine*, vol. 81, 2006, pp. 82–5.

25 www.betterhealth.vic.gov.au/bhcv2/bhcarticles.nsf/pages/Sleep?opendocument (retrieved 21 May 2010).

26 Haus, E. & Smolensky, M., 'Biological clocks and shift workers: Circadian dysregulation and potential long-term effects', *Cancer Causes and Control*, vol. 17, 2006, pp. 489–500.

27 Hassed, C., *The Essence of Health*, Ebury Press, Sydney, 2008, p. 78, and Dr Delwyn Bartlett, sleep psychologist, Woolcock Institute of Medical Research, Sydney, NSW, Australia: unpublished data collected on large groups at Prince Alfred Hospital between 2002 and 2006.

28 Hassed, *The Essence of Health*, and Bartlett, unpublished data.

29 www.stanford.edu/~dement/circadian.html (retrieved 21 May 2010).

30 Circadian Rhythm Information, www.stanford.edu/~dement/
circadian.html (retrieved 21 May 2010).

31 Ibid.

The Happy 100 Index

1 Bradburn, N.M., *The Structure of Psychological Well-being*, Aldine, Chicago,
1969, http://cloud9.norc.uchicago.edu/dlib/spwb/index.htm#bibinfo
(retrieved 14 May 2010).

2 Linley, P.A., Maltby, J., Wood, A.M. et al., 'Measuring happiness: The higher
order factor structure of subjective and psychological well-being measures',
Personality and Individual Differences, vol. 47, 2009, pp. 878–84.

3 Keyes, C.L.M., Shmotkin, D. & Ryff, C.D., 'Optimizing well-being: The
empirical encounter of two traditions', *Journal of Personality and Social
Psychology*, vol. 82, 2002, pp. 1007–22.

4 Cummins, R.A., Eckersley, R., Pallant, J. et al., 'Developing a national index
of subjective well-being: The Australian Unity Well-being Index', *Social
Indicators Research*, vol. 64, 2003, pp. 159–90.

5 Lovibond, S.H. & Lovibond, P.F., *Manual for the Depression Anxiety Stress
Scales*, Psychology Foundation of Australia, Sydney, 1995.

6 Tennant, R., Hiller, L., Fishwick, R. et al., 'The Warwick–Edinburgh Mental
Well-being Scale (WEMWBS): Development and UK validation', *Health and
Quality of Life Outcomes*, vol. 5, 2007, p. 63.

7 Diener, E., Emmons, R.A., Larsen, R.J. et al., 'The Satisfaction with Life
Scale', *Journal of Personality Assessment*, vol. 49, 1985, pp. 71–5.

8 Bradburn, *The Structure of Psychological Well-being*.

Step 1: Goals and values

1 Snyder, C.R., Rand, K.L. & Sigmon, D.R., 'Hope theory: A member of the
positive psychology family', in Snyder, C.R., Lopez, S.J. (eds), *Handbook of
Positive Psychology*, Oxford University Press, London, 2002, pp. 257–76.

2 Covey, S., *The Seven Habits of Highly Effective People*, Business Library,
Melbourne, 1990.

3 Hayes, S.C., 'Acceptance and commitment therapy, relational frame
theory, and the third wave of behavioral and cognitive therapies', *Behavior
Therapy*, vol. 35, 2004, pp. 639–65.

4   Ciarrochi, J. & Bailey, A., *A CBT Practitioner's Guide to ACT: How to Bridge the Gap Between Cognitive Behavioral Therapy and Acceptance and Commitment Therapy*, New Harbinger Publications, Oakland, CA, 2008.

5   Hyun, I., 'Authentic values and individual autonomy', *Journal of Value Inquiry*, vol. 35, 2001, pp. 195–208.

6   Sheldon, K.M. & Elliot, A.J., 'Not all personal goals are personal: Comparing autonomous and controlled reasons for goals as predictors of effort and attainment', *Personality and Social Psychology Bulletin*, vol. 24, 1998, pp. 546–57.

7   Sheldon, K.M. & Elliot, A.J., 'Goal striving, need satisfaction, and longitudinal well-being: The self-concordance model', *Journal of Personality and Social Psychology*, vol. 76, 1999, pp. 482–97.

8   Sheldon, K.M., Elliot, A.J., Ryan, R.M. et al., 'Self-concordance and subjective well-being in four cultures', *Journal of Cross-Cultural Psychology*, vol. 35, 2004, pp. 209–23.

9   Hamilton, C., *Carpe Diem? The Deferred Happiness Syndrome*, Australia Institute, Sydney, 2004.

Step 2: Random acts of kindness

1   Batson, C.D., 'Experimental tests for the existence of altruism', *PSA: Proceedings of the Biennial Meeting of the Philosophy of Science Association*, vol. 2, 1992, pp. 69–78.

2   Becker, G.S., 'A theory of social interactions', *Journal of Political Economy*, vol. 82, 1974, pp. 1063–93.

3   Andreoni, J., 'Impure altruism and donations to public goods: A theory of warm-glow giving', *Economic Journal*, vol. 100, 1990, pp. 467–77.

4   Bolton, G. & Ockenfels, A., 'ERC: A theory of equity, reciprocity and competition', *American Economic Review*, vol. 90, 2000, pp. 166–93.

5   Thompson, R., 'Self-serving altruism: Not an oxymoron', *Physician Executive*, vol. 33, 2007, pp. 82–3.

6   Isen, A.M. & Levin, P.F., 'Effect of feeling good on helping: Cookies and kindness', *Journal of Personality and Social Psychology*, vol. 21, 1972, pp. 384–8.

7   Batson, C.D., Coke, J.S., Chard, F. et al., 'Generality of the "glow of goodwill": Effects of mood on helping and information acquisition', *Social Psychology Quarterly*, vol. 42, 1979, pp. 176–9.

8   Weyant, J.M., 'Effects of mood states, costs, and benefits on helping', *Journal of Personality and Social Psychology*, vol. 36, 1978, pp. 1169–76.

9   Fishbach, A. & Labroo, A.A., 'Be better or be merry: How mood affects self-control', *Journal of Personality and Social Psychology*, vol. 93, 2007, pp. 158–73.

10 Schwartz, C., Meisenhelder, J.B., Ma, Y. et al., 'Altruistic social interest behaviors are associated with better mental health', *Psychosomatic Medicine*, vol. 65, 2003, pp. 778–85.

11 Conway, J.M., Rogelberg, S.G. & Pitts, V.E., 'Workplace helping: Interactive effects of personality and momentary positive affect', *Human Performance*, vol. 22, 2009, pp. 321–39.

12 Tsai, W.-C., Chen, C.-C. & Liu, H.-L., 'Test of a model linking employee positive moods and task performance', *Journal of Applied Psychology*, vol. 92, 2007, pp. 1570–83.

13 Rosenhan, D.L., Salovey, P. & Hargis, K., 'The joys of helping: Focus of attention mediates the impact of positive affect on altruism', *Journal of Personality and Social Psychology*, vol. 49, 1981, pp. 899–905.

14 Dunn, E.W., Aknin, L.B. & Norton, M.I., 'Spending money on others promotes happiness', *Science*, vol. 319, 2008, pp. 1687–8.

15 Moen, P., Dempster-McClain, D. & Williams, R.M., 'Social integration and longevity: An event history analysis of women's roles and resilience', *American Sociological Review*, vol. 45, 1989, pp. 635–47.

16 Wink, P. & Dillon, M., 'Do generative adolescents become healthy older adults?', in Post, S.G. (ed.), *Altruism and Health: Perspectives from Empirical Research*, Oxford University Press, Oxford, 2007, pp. 43–54.

17 Luoh, M.C. & Herzog, A.R., 'Individual consequences of volunteer and paid work in old age: Health and mortality', *Journal of Health and Social Behavior*, vol. 43, 2002, pp. 368–78.

18 McClelland, D., McClelland, D.C. & Kirchnit, C., 'The effect of motivational arousal through films on salivary immunoglobulin A', *Psychology and Health*, vol. 2, 1988, pp. 31–52.

19 Stebnicki, M.A., 'Empathy fatigue: Healing the mind, body, and spirit of professional counselors', *American Journal of Psychiatric Rehabilitation*, vol. 10, 2007, pp. 317–38.

20 Karylowski, J., 'Self-focused attention, prosocial norms and prosocial behavior', *Polish Psychological Bulletin*, vol. 10, 1979, pp. 57–66.

21 Huang, P.H. & Swedloff, R., 'Perspectives on lawyer happiness: Authentic happiness and meaning at law firms', *Syracuse Law Review*, vol. 58, 2008, pp. 335–50.

22 Anon., 'Random acts of kindness', 2010, http://medlibraryorg/medwiki/ Random_Acts_of_Kindness (retrieved 21 April 2010).

23 Lara, A., 'Random acts of senseless kindness', *San Francisco Chronicle*, 1991, 16 May.

24 Lyubomirsky, S., Tkach, C. & Yelverton, J., 'Pursuing sustained happiness through random acts of kindness and counting one's blessings: Test of two six-week interventions', unpublished data, University of California, Riverside, Department of Psychology, 2004.

25 Dean, B., 'Kindness and the case for altruism', *Authentic Happiness Newsletter*, 2006, www.authentichappiness.sas.upenn.edu/newsletter. aspx?id=70 (retrieved 21 April 2010).

26 The Random Acts of Kindness Foundation (www.actsofkindness.org) is a great online resource. Their work inspired some of the practical ideas presented here.

Step 3: Mindfulness

1   Hayes, S.C. & Wilson, K.G., 'Acceptance and commitment therapy: Altering the verbal support for experiential avoidance', *Behavior Analyst*, vol. 17, 1994, pp. 289–303.

2   Vowles, K.E., Wetherell, J.L. & Sorrell, J.T., 'Targeting acceptance, mindfulness, and values-based action in chronic pain: Findings of two preliminary trials of an outpatient group-based intervention', *Cognitive and Behavioral Practice*, vol. 16, 2009, pp. 49–58.

3   Petersen, C.L. & Zettle, R.D., 'Treating inpatients with comorbid depression and alcohol use disorders: A comparison of acceptance and commitment therapy versus treatment as usual', *Psychological Record*, vol. 59, 2009, pp. 521–36.

4   Paez, M.B., Luciano, C. & Gutierrez, O., 'Psychological treatment to cope with breast cancer: A comparative study between strategies of acceptance and cognitive control', *Psicooncologia*, vol. 4, 2007, pp. 75–95.

5   Hernandez-Lopez, M., Luciano, M., Bricker, J.B. et al., 'Acceptance and commitment therapy for smoking cessation: A preliminary study of its effectiveness in comparison with cognitive behavioral therapy', *Psychology of Addictive Behaviors*, vol. 23, 2009, pp. 723–30.

6   Powers, M.B., Zum Vorde Sive Vording, M.B. & Emmelkamp, P.M., 'Acceptance and commitment therapy: A meta-analytic review', *Psychotherapy and Psychosomatics*, vol. 78, 2009, pp. 73–80.

Step 4: Strengths and solutions

1   Dweck, C.S., *Mindset: The New Psychology of Success*, Random House, New York, 2006.

2   Crum, A.J. & Langer, E.J., 'Mindset matters: Exercise and the placebo effect', *Psychological Science*, vol. 18, 2007, pp. 165–71.

3   Peterson, C. & Seligman, M., *Character Strengths and Virtues: A Handbook and Classification*, Oxford University Press, Oxford, 2004.

4   Linley, P.A., *Average to A+: Realising Strengths in Yourself and Others*, CAPP Press, Coventry, UK, 2008.

5   Seligman, M.E., Steen, T.A., Park, N. et al., 'Positive psychology progress: Empirical validation of interventions', *American Psychologist*, vol. 60, 2005, pp. 410–21.

6   Grant, A.M., Curtayne, L. & Burton, G., 'Executive coaching enhances goal attainment, resilience and workplace well-being: A randomised controlled study', *Journal of Positive Psychology*, vol. 4, 2009, pp. 396–407.

7   Green, L.S., Grant, A.M. & Rynsaardt, J., 'Evidence-based life coaching for senior high school students: Building hardiness and hope', *International Coaching Psychology Review*, vol. 2, 2007, pp. 24–32.

8   Grant, A.M. & O'Connor, S.A. 'The differential effects of solution-focused and problem-focused coaching questions: A pilot study with implications for practice', *Industrial and Commercial Training*, vol. 42, 2010, pp. 102–11.

9   Szabo, P. & Meier, D., *Coaching Plain and Simple: Solution-focused Brief Coaching Essentials*. W.W. Norton & Co., New York, 2009, pp. xii, 109.

10 Grant, A.M. & Greene, J., *Coach Yourself*, Perseus Publishing, Cambridge, MA, 2001, pp. xciii, 211.

Step 5: Gratitude

1   Polak, E.L. & McCullough, M.E., 'Is gratitude an alternative to materialism?', *Journal of Happiness Studies*, 2006, vol. 7, pp. 343–60.

2   Watkins, P.C., Woodward, K., Stone, T. et al., 'Gratitude and happiness: Development of a measure of gratitude and relationships with subjective well-being', *Social Behavior and Personality*, vol. 31, 2003, pp. 431–52.

3   Wood, A.M., Joseph, S. & Maltby, J., 'Gratitude uniquely predicts satisfaction with life: Incremental validity above the domains and facets of the five-factor model', *Personality and Individual Differences*, vol. 45, 2008, pp. 49–54.

4   Algoe, S.B., Haidt, J. & Gable, S.L., 'Beyond reciprocity: Gratitude and relationships in everyday life', *Emotion*, vol. 8, 2008, pp. 425–9.

5   Tsang, J.-A., 'Gratitude and prosocial behaviour: An experimental test of gratitude', *Cognition and Emotion*, vol. 20, 2006, pp. 138–48.

6   McCullough, M.E., Kimeldorf, M.B. & Cohen, A.D., 'An adaptation for altruism? The social causes, social effects, and social evolution of gratitude', *Current Directions in Psychological Science*, vol. 17, 2008, pp. 281–5.

7   Brdar, I. & Kashdan, T.B., 'Character strengths and well-being in Croatia: An empirical investigation of structure and correlates', *Journal of Research in Personality*, 2009, np.

8   Shimai, S., Otake, K., Park, N. et al., 'Convergence of character strengths in American and Japanese young adults', *Journal of Happiness Studies*, vol. 7, 2006, pp. 311–22.

9   Naito, T., Wangwan, J. & Tani, M., 'Gratitude in university students in Japan and Thailand', *Journal of Cross-cultural Psychology*, vol. 36, 2005, pp. 247–63.

10 Park, N., Peterson, C. & Seligman, M.E., 'Character strengths in fifty-four nations and the fifty US states', *Journal of Positive Psychology*, vol. 1, 2006, pp. 118–29.

11 Wood, A.M., Joseph, S., Lloyd, J. et al., 'Gratitude influences sleep through the mechanism of pre-sleep cognitions', *Journal of Psychosomatic Research*, vol. 66, 2009, pp. 43–8.

12 Palmatier, R.W., Jarvis, C.B., Bechkoff, J.R. et al., 'The role of customer gratitude in relationship marketing', *Journal of Marketing*, vol. 73, 2009, pp. 1–18.

13 Yanmei, W., 'Cultivating positive emotions and well-being: Recording happy events and expressing gratitude', *Psychological Science* (China), vol. 32, 2009, pp. 598–600.

14 Seligman, Steen, Park et al., 'Positive psychology progress'.

15 Helgeson, V.S., Reynolds, K.A. & Tomich, P.L., 'A meta-analitic view of benefit finding and growth', *Journal of Consulting and Clinical Psychology*, vol. 74, 2006, pp. 797–816.

16 Stanton, A.L., Danoff-Burg, S., Sworowski, L.A. et al., 'Randomized, controller trial of written emotional expression and benefit finding in breast cancer patients', *Journal of Clinical Oncology*, vol. 20, 2002, pp. 4160–8.

17 Bower, J.E., Moskowitz, J.T. & Epel, E., 'Is benefit finding good for your health?', *Current Directions in Psychological Science*, vol. 18, 2009, pp. 337–41.

18 Ibid.

19 Seligman, Steen, Park et al., 'Positive Psychology progress'.
20 Peterson, C., *A Primer in Positive Psychology*, Oxford University Press, New York, 2006, pp. viii, 386.

Step 6: Forgiveness

1 Maltby, J., Day, L. & Barber, L., 'Forgiveness and happiness: The differing contexts of forgiveness using the distinction between hedonic and eudaimonic happiness', *Journal of Happiness Studies*, vol. 6, 2005, pp. 1–13.
2 Cosgrove, L. & Konstam, V., 'Forgiveness and forgetting: Clinical implications for mental health counselors', *Journal of Mental Health Counseling*, vol. 30, 2008, pp. 1–13.
3 Murphy, J.E., 'Forgiveness and resentment', *Midwest Studies in Philosophy*, vol. 7, 1982, pp. 503–16.
4 van Oyen Witvliet, C., Ludwig, T.E. & Vander Lann, K.L., 'Granting forgiveness or harboring grudges: Implications for emotion, physiology, and health', *Psychological Science*, vol. 12, 2001, pp. 117–23.
5 Worthington, E., Witvliet, C., Pietrini, P. et al., 'Forgiveness, health, and well-being: A review of evidence for emotional versus decisional forgiveness, dispositional forgivingness, and reduced unforgiveness', *Journal of Behavioral Medicine*, vol. 30, 2007, pp. 291–302.
6 Kearns, J.N. & Fincham, F.D., 'Victim and perpetrator accounts of interpersonal transgressions: Self-serving or relationship-serving biases?', *Personality and Social Psychology Bulletin*, vol. 31, 2005, pp. 321–33.
7 Worthington, Witvliet, Pietrini et al., 'Forgiveness, health, and well-being'.
8 Konstam, V., Marx, F., Schurer, J. et al., 'Forgiving: What mental health counselors are telling us', *Journal of Mental Health Counseling*, vol. 22, 2000, pp. 253–67.

Step 7: Social networks

1 Kahneman, D., Krueger, A.B., Schkade, D.A. et al., 'A survey method for characterizing daily life experience: The day reconstruction method', *Science*, vol. 306, 2004, pp. 1776–80.
2 Michael, Y.L., Berkman, L.F. & Kawachi, I., 'Living arrangements, social integration and change in functional health status', *American Journal of Epidemiology*, vol. 153, 2001, pp. 123–31.
3 Cacioppo, J.T., Fowler J.H. & Christakis, N.A., 'Alone in the crowd: The structure and spread of loneliness in a large social network', *Journal of Personality and Social Psychology*, vol. 97, 2009, pp. 977–91.

4 Cacioppo, J.T. & Patrick, W., *Loneliness: Human Nature and the Need for Social Connection*, W.W. Norton & Co., New York, 2008.

5 Eisenberger, N.I. & Lieberman, M.D., 'Why rejection hurts: A common neural alarm system for physical and social pain', *Trends in Cognitive Sciences*, vol. 8, 2004, pp. 294–300.

6 Eisenberger, N.I., Lieberman, M.D. & Williams, K.D., 'Does rejection hurt? An fMRI study of social exclusion', *Science*, vol. 302, 2003, pp. 290–2.

7 Capsi, A., Harrington, H., Moffitt, T.E. et al., 'Socially isolated children 20 years later: Risk of cardiovascular disease', *Archives of Pediatric and Adolescent Medicine*, vol. 357, 2006, pp. 307–79.

8 Cacioppo, Fowler & Christakis, 'Alone in the crowd'.

9 McPherson, M., Smith-Lovin, L. & Brashears, M.E., 'Social isolation in America: Changes in core discussion networks over two decades', *American Sociological Review*, vol. 71, 2006, pp. 353–75.

10 Flood, M., *Mapping Loneliness in Australia*, Australia Institute, Sydney, 2005.

11 Cacioppo, Fowler & Christakis, 'Alone in the crowd'.

12 Lukes, S., *Emile Durkheim, His Life and Work: A Historical and Critical Study*, Stanford University Press, Stanford, CA, 1985.

13 Burt, R.S., 'A note on strangers, friends and happiness', *Social Networks*, vol. 9, 1987, pp. 311–31.

14 Eyal, T. & Epley, N., 'How to seem telepathic: Enabling mind reading by matching construal', *Psychological Science*, vol. 21, no. 5, 2010, pp. 700–5.

15 Boginski, V., Butenko, S., Pardalos, P.M. et al., 'Social networks in sports', 2004 http://ise.tamu.edu/People/faculty/butenko/papers/nba_graph.pdf (retrieved 28 April 2010)

16 Burt, 'A note on strangers, friends and happiness'.

17 Eyal & Epley, 'How to seem telepathic'.

18 Pugh, D.S., 'Service with a smile: Emotional contagion in the service encounter', *Academy of Management Journal*, vol. 44, 2001, pp. 1018–27.

19 Cialdini, R., *Influence: Science and Practice*, Allyn & Bacon, London, 2001.

20 Fowler J.H. & Christakis, N.A., 'Dynamic spread of happiness in a large social network: Longitudinal analysis over 20 years in the Framingham Heart Study', *British Medical Journal*, vol. 338, 2008, pp. 24–7.

21 Christakis, N.A. & Fowler J.H., *Connected: The Surprising Power of Our Social Networks and How They Shape Our Lives*, Little, Brown & Co., New York, 2009.

Step 8: Reflect, review, renew

1   Gogbet, F. & Clarkson, G., 'Chunks in expert memory: Evidence for the magical number four ... or it is two?', *Memory*, vol. 12, 2004, pp. 732–47.

2   Vohs, K., Baumeister, R., Schmeichel, B. et al., 'Making choices impairs subsequent self-control: A limited-resource account of decision making, self-regulation, and active initiative', *Journal of Personality and Social Psychology*, vol. 94, 2008, pp. 883–98.

3   Flaherty, A.W., 'Frontotemporal and dopaminergic control of idea generation and creative drive', *Journal of Comparative Neurology*, vol. 493, 2005, pp. 147–53.

4   Wapner, J., 'Blogging—It's good for you', *Scientific American*, June 2008, www.scientificamerican.com/article.cfm?id=the-healthy-type (retrieved 23 May 2010).

5   Klein, K. & Boals, A., 'Expressive writing can increase working memory capacity', *Journal of Experimental Psychology*, vol. 130, 2001, pp. 520–33.

6   Baikie, K.A. & Wilhelm, K., 'Emotional and physical health benefits of expressive writing', *Advances in Psychiatric Treatment*, vol. 11, 2005, pp. 338–46.

7   Conway, J.M., Rogelberg, S.G. & Pitts, V.E., 'Workplace helping: Interactive effects of personality and momentary positive affect', *Human Performance*, vol. 22, 2009, pp. 321–39.

8   McClelland, McClelland & Kirchnit, 'The effect of motivational arousal through films on salivary immunoglobulin A'.

9   Brdar, I. & Kashdan, T.B., 'Character strengths and well-being in Croatia: An empirical investigation of structure and correlates', *Journal of Research in Personality*, 2009, np. Shimai, S., Otake, K., Park, N. et al., 'Convergence of character strengths in American and Japanese young adults', *Journal of Happiness Studies*, vol. 7, 2006, pp. 311–22.

10 Wood, A.M., Joseph, S., Lloyd, J. et al., 'Gratitude influences sleep through the mechanism of pre-sleep cognitions', *Journal of Psychosomatic Research*, vol. 66, 2009, pp. 43–8.

11 Palmatier, R.W., Jarvis, C.B., Bechkoff, J.R. et al., 'The role of customer gratitude in relationship marketing', *Journal of Marketing*, vol. 73, 2009, pp. 1–18.

12 Seligman, Steen, Park et al., 'Positive psychology progress'.

13 Clark, A., 'Forgiveness: A neurological model', *Medical Hypotheses*, vol. 64, 2005, pp. 649–54.

14 Worthington, Witvliet, Pietrini et al., 'Forgiveness, health, and well-being'.

15 Harris, A., Luskin, F., Norman, S. et al., 'Effects of a group forgiveness intervention on forgiveness, perceived stress, and trait-anger', *Journal of Clinical Psychology*, vol. 62, 2006, pp. 715–33.

16 Cacioppo & Patrick, *Loneliness*.

17 Pugh, 'Service with a smile'.

18 Fowler & Christakis, 'Dynamic spread of happiness in a large social network'.

19 Ozer, D.J. & Benet-Martinez, V., 'Personality and the prediction of consequential outcomes', *Annual Review of Psychology*, vol. 57, 2006, pp. 401–21.

20 Pennebaker, J.W., 'Writing about emotional experiences as a therapeutic process', *Psychological Science*, vol. 8, 1997, pp. 162–6.

21 Baikie & Wilhelm, 'Emotional and physical health benefits of expressive writing'.

22 Ibid.

23 Boud, D., 'Using journal writing to enhance reflective practice', *New Directions for Adult and Continuing Education*, vol. 90, 2001, pp. 9–17.

24 Frisina ,P., Borod, J. & Lepore, S., 'A meta-analysis of the effects of written emotional disclosure on the health outcomes of clinical populations', *Journal of Nervous and Mental Disease*, vol. 192, 2004, pp. 629–34.

The science

1 Eid & Larsen (eds), *The Science of Subjective Well-Being*, pp. xiii, 546.

2 Cummins, Eckersley, Pallant et al., 'Developing a national index of subjective well-being'.

3 Hassed, *The Essence of Health*.

4 Sensewear information can be found at www.sensewear.com/default.php.

5 Reiter, R.J., Paredes, S.D., Manchester, L.C. et al., 'Reducing oxidative/ nitrosative stress: A newly discovered genre for melatonin', *Critical Reviews in Biochemistry and Molecular Biology*, vol. 44, 2009, pp. 175–200.

6 Kanishi, Y., Kobayashi, Y., Noda, S. et al., 'Differential growth inhibitory effect of melatonin on two endometrial cancer cell lines', *Journal of Pineal Research*, vol. 28, 2000, pp. 227–33.

7 Hassed, *The Essence of Health*.

8 Ibid.

9 Irwin, M. & Vedhara, K., *Human Psychoneuroimmunology*, Oxford University Press, Oxford, 2005.

10 Rein, G., Atkinson, M. & McCraty, M., 'The physiological and psychological effects of compassion and anger', *Journal of Advancement in Medicine*, vol. 8, 1995, pp. 87–105.

11 McClelland, McClelland & Kirchnit, 'The effect of motivational arousal through films on salivary immunoglobulin A'.

12 Fredrickson, B.L., 'What good are positive emotions?', *Review of General Psychology*, vol. 2, 1998, pp. 300–19.

13 Tugade, M.M. & Fredrickson, B.L., 'Resilient individuals use positive emotions to bounce back from negative emotional experiences', *Journal of Personality and Social Psychology*, vol. 86, 2004, pp. 320–33.

14 Berg, C.J., Snyder, C.R. & Hamilton, N., 'The effectiveness of a hope intervention in coping with cold pressor pain', *Journal of Health Psychology*, vol. 13, 2008, pp. 804–9.

15 Lutz, A., Greischar, L.L., Rawlings, N.B. et al., 'Long-term meditators self-induce high-amplitude gamma synchrony during mental practice', *Proceedings of the National Academy of Sciences of the United States of America*, vol. 101, 2004, pp. 16369–73.

16 Blood, A., Zatorre, R., Bermudez, P. et al., 'Emotional responses to pleasant and unpleasant music correlate with activity in paralimbic brain regions', *Nature Neuroscience*, vol. 2, 1999, pp. 382–7.

17 Orme-Johnson, D., Schneider, R., Son, Y. et al., 'Neuroimaging of meditation's effect on brain reactivity to pain', *Neuroreport*, vol. 17, 2006, pp. 1359–63.

Index

Eight Steps to Happiness journal

Use this space as the beginning of your happiness journal, to draft your 'letter from the future', or simply to take down thoughts and observations as you read.